JESUS CAN...
GIVE YOU PURPOSE

Christian Writers Collective, LLC
Stephanie K. Reynolds, Founder

Jesus Can...Give You Purpose
Copyright © 2024 by Christian Writers Collective, LLC
Stephanie K. Reynolds, Founder

All rights reserved. No parts of this publication may be reproduced, stored in a retrieval system, or transmitted in any form or by any means—electronic, mechanical, photocopying, recording, scanning or other—except for brief quotations in critical reviews or articles, without the prior written permission of the publisher.

Scripture quotations are from the King James Version unless otherwise noted.

Scriptures marked NIV are taken from THE HOLY BIBLE: New International Version ©1978 by the New York International Bible Society, used by permission of Zondervan Bible Publishers.

Scriptures marked NKJV are taken from the New King James Version®. Copyright © 1982 by Thomas Nelson, Inc. Used by permission. All rights reserved.

Scriptures marked NASB are taken from the New American Standard Bible, Copyright ©1960, 1962, 1963, 1968, 1971, 1973, 1975, 1977 by The Lockman Foundation.

Book cover design by Virtually Possible Designs

ISBN 979-8-9862076-4-3 (paperback)
ISBN 979-8-9862076-5-0 (e-book)

Jesus Can . . . Give You Purpose
is dedicated
to Willie C. Reynolds,
the best dad in the world.
He went home to heaven
at ninety-one years old.

Intermingled throughout the book you hold in your hands, you will find stories of how lives were changed by Jesus. *Jesus Can . . . Give You Purpose* contains stories of people who have found purpose in their lives through following Christ as well as testimonies from forty-six Christian writers who came to know Jesus as their Lord and Savior.

Testimonies are denoted with a symbol of a cross. Stories of purpose are denoted with a bullseye. Our prayer is that you find Jesus within the pages of this book.

Table of Contents

A 🎯 denotes a story of purpose
A ✝ denotes a testimony of salvation

Introduction xiii

1. My Sweet Season of Purpose as Steve's Mom 🎯
   by Stephanie Reynolds 1

2. It's Not All About Me 🎯
   by Kitty Foth-Regner...7

3. My Sweet Spot Began with Prayer ✝ 🎯
   by Nyla Kay Wilkerson 13

4. Our Painful Gauntlet, God's Precious Grace ✝
   by Elic 17

5. A Rapper's Tragedy and Triumph ✝
   by Adrian Moore..23

6. Love Conquers Fears ✝ 🎯
   by Jane Jackson...29

7. The Everlasting Impact of Billy Graham ✝
   by Kenyon Ross...35

8. Loving the Little People 🎯
   by Samantha Gilson...41

9. Left for Dead, But Now Alive Forevermore ✝
   by Isaiah 45

10 Living in the Shadow 🎯
    by Kim Patterson 49

11 Loved with an Everlasting Love ✝
    by Linda Holmes 55

12 From Cambodia's Killing Fields to Alabama's Lumber Yards, and Back ✝
    by Long Kuoy 59

13 No Longer a Lost Cause ✝
    by Ronnie Blanton 65

14 My Rescue Story ✝ 🎯
    by Stephen J. Miller 69

15 Lost but Found and Free Forevermore ✝
    by Tha Taw Wah 75

16 From Death to Life ✝
    by Sara Davison 81

17 God's Handiwork in Beautiful, Hearing Impaired Friends ✝ 🎯
    by Joshua Asuela 85

18 From Brokenness to a Vibrant New Life ✝
    by Kelly Erickson 89

19 A New Creation ✝
    by Karen R. Naidl 95

20 Making Music for my Maker ✝ 🎯
by Luke Riesterer 99

21 God as My "Why" ✝ 🎯
by Lauren McNeese 103

22 Chosen by the King of Kings ✝
by Beth Paraiso 107

23 A Serendipitous Life of Giving Back ✝ 🎯
by Michael Shepherd 111

24 The Last Page ✝
by Jack Urban 117

25 God's Story in my Life ✝
by Desiree Taylor 121

26 Journey to my Purpose ✝ 🎯
by Cheri Swalwell 125

27 Waking up from the Longest Dream ✝
by Marlayne Giron 129

28 Why Am I Here? And What's Next? 🎯
by RuthAnn Gumm 133

29 Who Is My King, and What Is He Saying? ✝ 🎯
by Mary Emily Mulloy 139

30 I Just Knew ✝
by Carolyn Miller 145

31 Father to the Fatherless ✝ 🎯
by Harriet Okumu 149

32 Living to Love ✝
by Bob Mulloy 153

33 Football, Faith, and the Sovereignty of God ✝
by David Naidl 159

34 Is That All There Is? 🎯
by James Koenig 163

35 A Senior's Journey to Salvation ✝
by Gregg Bates 169

36 A Daughter of Promise, a Warrior in Prayer ✝
by Betzabé 173

37 Bringing Light Through Literacy ✝ 🎯
by C.C. 179

38 My Father's Love Changes Everything ✝
by Danilo Chacon 183

39 Running with the Devil Versus
Walking with the Savior ✝ 🎯
by Dorsey McDonald 189

40 Saved and Kept by Grace ✝
by Ernesto Rivas 193

41 My Journey ✝
   by Eymy Chacon 199

42 Born as a Refugee, Born Again as a Son ✝
   by Ger 203

43 Our Heavenly Father Always Watches Out for Us ✝
   by Norman Chacon 207

44 The Secret Is His Righteousness ✝ 🎯
   by Phil Snyder 213

45 Buried for Three Days but Spared and Serving the Savior ✝
   by Myrlande Laurent 219

46 Destiny Dream 🎯
   by Tom Donnan 225

Closing Comments 231

Other books in the *Jesus Can . . .* Series

Jesus Can...Give You a New Life

Jesus Can...Heal Your Hurts

Jesus Can...Show You the Truth, Coming April 2025

Jesus Can...Love You Through Your Pain, Coming October 2025

Introducing...
Jesus Can Give a Helping Hand Fund

For every copy that you purchase, 10% of this book's net profits for two years will be given to an organization or individual that shares our primary mission: to spread the Gospel far and wide.

Our first honoree for this grant was an easy and obvious choice: Literacy & Evangelism International (LEI), located near Atlanta, Georgia, and staffed by missionaries Bob and Mary Mulloy.

The selection of LEI was easy because twenty-nine of the forty-six articles in this book are testimonies from individuals served by or affiliated with LEI. Bob and Mary's testimonies are counted among them.

Atlanta is the ideal location for LEI because it is the home to the Hartsfield Jackson International Airport (ATL), the world's busiest airport. Many of the people arriving at ATL from over 150 nations choose to make metro Atlanta their new home. As evidenced by the writers in CWC Book 3, Bob and Mary have had the opportunity for sixteen years to minister to many individuals, including three writers in Book 3—a victim of violence in Africa, an escapee from the killing fields of Cambodia, and a Haitian woman who was buried alive for three days.

It is our prayer that this grant will help them serve the diverse mission field in Atlanta for many more years, for it's in Jesus' name that we pray.

If you'd like to support Bob and Mary's work at LEI directly, you can also send a donation to: Literacy & Evangelism International, 1800 S. Jackson Ave, Tulsa, OK 74107. If you do so, please write "For the ministry of Bob and Mary Mulloy" on the memo line of the check.

Thank you for participating in the mission of spreading the Gospel far and wide!

—*Stephanie*

Introduction

"Complicated" is the only single word that comes close to accurately describing my relationship with my dad for the last five years of his life. Rewarding, exhausting, exasperating, nurturing, but forever loving and praying always sum up that precious time.

What is absolutely clear is that caring for my dad, when dementia left him unable to care for himself, was God's purpose for my life in 2023. Publishing this book would have to wait.

But they that wait upon the LORD shall renew their strength; they shall mount up with wings as eagles; they shall run, and not be weary; and they shall walk, and not faint (Isaiah 40:31).

It would take another book to record the multitude of blessings that I received as a result of waiting on the Lord's timing for publishing this book a year later than originally planned. Below are a few of the highlights…

- Bob Mulloy - Bob and his wife, Mary, serve as missionaries to immigrants in the metro Atlanta area. Bob first heard about the *Jesus Can* series during a 6 am online prayer group, in which we both participate, and collected testimonies for this book from around the world.

- Harriet Okumu's beautifully written testimony that was submitted on the last day, July 4, 2024.

- Prayer warriors - Nyla Kay, Vivienne, and the 6 am Prayer Group at my church, just to name a few.

- RuthAnn Gumm - the CWC's own Energizer Bunny, bringing all the pieces of Book 3 together with the same anointed speed and perseverance as the Israelites rebuilding the wall in the book of Nehemiah.

• My dad, Willie C. Reynolds - This book is dedicated to him because he went to heaven in February 2024, leaving behind a legacy of living life on purpose for ninety-one years. He also initiated a financial legacy for our family that allowed me to fund my God-given dream of helping other Christians to fund their God-given dreams.

If our heavenly Father is calling you to share your testimony in the next book of the Jesus Can Series, please listen. You can go to the Share Your Story page of our website, JesusCanBookSeries.com, for more information.

To God be the glory!

—*Stephanie*

1

◎ My Sweet Season of Purpose as Steve's Mom

▼

by Stephanie Reynolds
CWC Founder

Several factors made our Thursday prayer extra special last week. The combination of all of these factors made it an amazing day, indeed. First, I should explain that RuthAnn Gumm, a CWC writer, member, and one of the primary editors of this particular book, and I have been praying over the phone at 8 am on most Thursdays for more years than we can remember. But we're guessing that it's been at least three. Praying through good times and bad for our families and the Christian Writers Collective, LLC (CWC) has forged an extraordinary bond between the two of us even though we've never met in person.

The realization of how many years we'd been praying is one of the factors that made last Thursday remarkable. Another was the fact that last Thursday was the 4th of July—the anniversary of our country's Declaration of Independence—the 248th birthday of the United States of America. This prompted me to share another remarkable thing about the 4th of July with my friend, RuthAnn: it's my son, Steven's, spiritual birthday. He was born again when he asked Jesus to come into his heart and save him on July 4, 1988. We celebrated his thirty-sixth spiritual birthday this year. He made this life-changing decision at the ripe old age of four. It was my pleasure to recall these precious memories with RuthAnn.

Even though it's thirty-six years later, the newsreel-like video of my son's salvation vividly replays in my mind as if it had happened yesterday. I remember the Holy Spirit prompting me to talk to my son about his need to be saved in the spring of 1988. A few weeks later, when the opportunity arose, our first conversation was brief. Everything was going okay until I told Steve that the first step toward being saved was recognizing that he was a sinner, just like every other human being that was born on earth. Our talk was over when Steve matter-of-factly told me, "I'm no sinner, Mom."

When the 4th of July arrived, less than a week later, it was Steve who reopened our conversation. We had enjoyed a long day of picnicking in the park and watching fireworks with our friends. The kids were so tired that they went to bed without any of the usual stalls of needing to go to the bathroom or wanting a hug, bedtime story, or drink of water. However, shortly after I turned out the lights and said goodnight, my exhausted son got out of his bed and ran into my arms, crying. It was impossible to console his chest-heaving tears as he struggled to get out his words. He was begging me to pray with him. He wanted me to help him to tell Jesus that he now knew that he was a sinner, and he wanted to be saved. I don't remember the exact words of his prayer, but I'll never forget how Steve and I both were forever changed by his heartfelt plea. God confirmed that being Steve's mom was His purpose for that season of my life when He used me to show my son how to receive His free gift of eternal life.

I finished sharing this precious memory with RuthAnn by telling her how God's gift to me was to confirm that my son really had been born again at such a young age. While it was still summer, Steve and I were driving alone together in my car. Suddenly, Steve asked me about the song that was playing on the radio. He said, "Mom, is that a godly song?" My short and honest reply was, "No." His instant response was, "Then why are you listening to it?" With a combination of embarrassment, motherly pride, and Holy Spirit-filled joy, I immediately turned the dial to our local Christian radio station.

My son is now forty years old. His active, but humble walk with the Lord still inspires me. As you'll find posted on our website, my son was also part of the inspiration that led me to found this business/ministry. He took on the responsibility of becoming the primary breadwinner for our family of two when he was just seventeen years old. Since then, I have been praying and working toward fulfilling the parental duty that I see set forth in Proverbs 13:22. This verse says that we are to leave an inheritance for our children's children.

I believe that God called me to the business/ministry of publishing Christian books not only to spread the gospel and to help fund the God-given dreams of our writers, but because Steve is an excellent writer. His skill as a gifted writer also became apparent when he was just four years old.

Jesus Can...

My dream, my purpose, and my prayer is to see my son doing what he does best: serving our heavenly Father as a writer. This I pray in Jesus' name. Amen.

Give You Purpose

Stephanie Reynolds, CWC Founder

2

It's Not All About Me

by Kitty Foth-Regner
www.EverlastingPlace.com

For the first forty-seven years of my life, I had just one purpose: achieving, maintaining, and enhancing my personal happiness. My guiding principle? What matters in this life is me. It's all about me. I am all that matters.

In my defense, I came by this notion honestly. It blossomed in the culture of the 1960s, as I was, at least in theory, becoming an adult. Nouveau Narcissism was tough to resist, especially against the backdrop of the pop music we adored. I could cite many pertinent titles, but perhaps the most blatant was Whitney Houston's "Greatest Love of All," written by singer/songwriter Linda Creed and first recorded in 1977 by George Benson. Ponder this song's lyrics, which insist that the greatest love is loving yourself.

Decades later, I would learn that self-love permeates the Bible's accounts of man's ancient rebellion against his Creator. And nothing has changed since then. As Solomon, the wisest man who ever lived, proclaimed in Ecclesiastes 1:9, "There's nothing new under the sun."

In fact, my generation's music gave lyrics and melody to many of the Bible's observations about man's basest instincts. Let me give you just two examples: "Is That All There Is?" was 1969's musical answer to "Let us eat and drink, for tomorrow we die" (Isaiah 22:13). And Frank Sinatra's 1969 hit "My Way" was a first-person expression of "Everyone did what was right in his own eyes" (Judges 17:6, e.g.).

It all added up to the fulfillment of a particularly stunning Bible prophecy—one that begins, "But know this, that in the last days perilous times will come: For men will be lovers of themselves ..." (2 Timothy 3:1-2). At any rate, I was all in on this thinking until I met Jesus Christ. Then, suddenly, my sorry attitude began to change.

It started in 2000, following the death of my beloved Christian mother. That was when I began searching for the truth about whether she might still exist somewhere out there. I analyzed every other major faith in the hope of finding truth in something less restrictive than Christianity. Failing that, I finally turned to the Bible, and to my utter amazement found it to be truth—as in absolute truth, the inspired and inerrant word of the God who created the heavens and the earth and everything in them. I responded by repenting of my sin and receiving Jesus Christ as my Savior. Then, as I studied this Bible, I learned slowly but surely that our purpose in life is not our own happiness, not our own pleasure, but to glorify God and advance His kingdom. Towards that end, we are actually to die to self.

Jesus Himself said so many different ways, personally and via His disciples. Just one example:

> *If anyone desires to come after Me, let him deny himself, and take up his cross daily, and follow Me. For whoever desires to save his life will lose it, but whoever loses his life for My sake will save it. For what profit is it to a man if he gains the whole world, and is himself destroyed or lost?* (Luke 9:23b-25, NKJV)

Strangely, He had started making these changes in me just as soon as I began seeking truth—not against my will, but in spite of it. Within a week after my mother's death, I'd become a volunteer at her nursing home. I began spending my Sundays making flower arrangements from my garden and on my Mondays delivering them to elderly residents. As summer and fall inevitably gave way to winter, I replaced the fresh materials with silk flowers, and the women and men I visited became dear friends.

Even stranger, whether or not I enjoyed this activity was, almost from the start, completely irrelevant. I was still a freelance copywriter, working enough to help pay the mortgage, and still a wife wanting to keep her husband happy. But I now had an irresistible purpose in life, a purpose that transcended every earthly responsibility and pleasure.

Over the years, my nursing-home work evolved into a true ministry, with lengthy weekly visits, monthly Christian Music Hours, and weekly Bible studies. What's more, I teamed up with a similarly minded friend at church, and together we expanded this ministry to two other nursing homes. I even wrote and published *The Song of Sadie Sparrow,* a novel set in an imaginary long-term care facility, and that book has reportedly inspired others to start their own ministries to the elderly.

Unfortunately, the COVID pandemic had dire consequences for nursing homes and nursing-home ministries. And so the Holy Spirit has led us all in new directions of service to glorify God and advance His kingdom.

But this underlying truth remains the same: Jesus Christ gives me purpose in life, and He is eager to do the same for you.

> *Ask, and it will be given to you; seek, and you will find; knock, and it will be opened to you. For everyone who asks receives, and he who seeks finds, and to him who knocks it will be opened* (Matthew 7:7-8).

Kitty Foth-Regner

Kitty Foth-Regner spent her forty year copywriting career specializing in scientific subjects. So, it is no surprise that it was the Bible's scientific truth that led her to Christ—a journey she recounted in her memoir *Heaven Without Her*. A long-term care volunteer since 2000, she's also published *The Song of Sadie Sparrow*, a novel exploring the relationships of three women whose paths cross in an idyllic nursing home.

Visit her at www.EverlastingPlace.com.

3

🎯 ✝ *My Sweet Spot Began with Prayer*

▼

by Nyla Kay Wilkerson

For I know the plans I have for you, declares the Lord... (Jeremiah 29:11).

The Bible teaches that God has a plan and purpose for each one of us. We are not randomly placed on earth. He has something for each one of us to do. Have you figured out what your purpose is?

I knew at an early age my purpose was to serve other people. Time and time again, God has made that clear. When my father died I was in elementary school, and I knew it was my responsibility to help care for my younger sister and my mother. My heart also felt the pull to offer comfort to my paternal grandparents by spending more time with them even though they lived 100 miles away.

As I got older, I realized that caring for others was only part of my purpose. The other part was to share Jesus with those I met. I would include in my prayers a request that each day God would use me to help someone. I wanted them to see His love through my actions. By opening myself up, I found a multitude of ways I could help. When family members stayed overnight in the hospital, I offered to stay with them. If someone was sick, I offered a meal. These tasks were not burdens and always done through love. They never felt like an obligation. I truly wanted to help.

My husband was divorced when we started dating. At that time his children were aged two and seven. I adored them and could tell they needed special attention to get through the break-up of their parents. We went on picnics, hikes, day trips, and church on Sunday mornings. The kids flourished. After the elementary Sunday School teacher at church retired, my daughter was afraid to go back. She was shy and did not know who was going to replace the teacher. After praying about how to ease her mind, I felt led to teach the class myself. That did the trick, and she eagerly went. Both kids became active in the Youth Group. I am thrilled to say they have each accepted Jesus as their Savior and been baptized into the Christian faith. My husband told me multiple times that he knew God put us together to lead the kids to salvation and give them a happy life.

My life has always revolved around serving others and sharing Jesus. I watched my nieces for a time while my sister worked. It was my pleasure to not only babysit but also drive them to preschool, practice, and appointments or my nephew to his. It gave me time to talk and sing about Jesus with them.

Helping my parents was a total pleasure. They had done so much for us. We lived close to each other, so I made meals, shared garden yields, and did whatever I could to make their lives easier. My parents were strong in their faith and taught me how to serve others anonymously. I always felt in my sweet spot when I made someone's life easier.

In this season of my life, God has called me to be a prayer warrior. I am older now and not able to do the things that I did in the past. When I pray, I ask God to put someone in my path or on my mind who needs me to be a blessing to them. Perhaps they need help paying a bill or getting groceries. Maybe I could assist them in writing a review or providing a reference. Sometimes just being available to chat is what is needed.

My purpose is still to help people but in a different way. I can best serve and care for others by interceding for them through prayer. Taking their needs to the Father on their behalf is powerful. I cannot count the many times I have been blessed by people that have done this for me.

Do you have a desire to help or serve others? The best place to start is on your knees and talking to God in prayer. It all began with a prayer to be used by God for His purpose for me. That could be your starting point too.

> *First of all, then, I urge that entreaties and prayers, petitions and thanksgivings, be made on behalf of all men* (I Timothy 2:1).

Nyla Kay Wilkerson

Nyla Kay is a follower of Jesus and a prayer warrior. A retired Christian bookstore owner and Sunday School teacher, she now reviews books, writes Christian blogs, (abbasprayerwarriorprincess@wordpress), co-blogs on HeartWingsBlog (heartwingsblog.com), guests on CheerUp! podcast, and is writing a novel. She has published one cookbook and contributes to *Guideposts*. Her hobbies include writing, cooking, gardening, and reading. A widow, she resides in Indiana with her two pets.

4

✝ *Our Painful Gauntlet God's Precious Grace*

▼

by Elic

First, I apologize for my English. It's my fourth language, and I must study it more. I was born in 1984 in Myanmar, also called Burma. My parents believe the Bible, as do most of our people in the Karen ethnic group (pop. over 5 million). I've always remembered my father's daily prayers and have tried to follow his caring counsel.

Myanmar's dictatorship has done ethnic cleansing on my people for more than seven decades. Life has been very hard for us. When I was a teen, I had to do heavy labor like searching for wood in the jungle and bringing it home. Some of the bundles weighed more than 100 pounds. After you do that for ten years, your body breaks down.

Life was painful for my family because my mother was usually sick, and my dad was disabled since age thirty-five when a tree fell and broke his hip. He was working alone, so that was a very bad day and long night alone for him.

Dad has great convictions and trained me to be strong. Sometimes he would send me to the jungle at night with only a candle to borrow rice from a neighbor. I had to do much cooking for my ten siblings and also do my schoolwork. Dad made us memorize Bible verses which I didn't like, but as I got older some of those promises came back when I really needed them.

When I was twelve years old, soldiers from the Burmese military burned down our village and all the fields around it. They shot all the animals and some people. My family had to run and hide in the jungle for ten days as the soldiers were planting landmines between the burnt houses and our gardens. That was our only land, so after a while some people moved back there; some died when they stepped on the landmines. Some of our village elders found buried mines and tried to disarm them. A few accidentally exploded and left these elders blind. Other men, like my uncle, needed to work in their gardens. He stepped on a mine and lost his leg. He has a prosthesis and is with us now in Atlanta, but it is hard for him to get a full-time job.

After hiding in the jungle for ten days, my family came out, and moved to another village for six years. In middle school I had to walk three hours every day to get to school and three hours home. I cannot describe some of those situations when I was alone. Often I had nightmares. I didn't know if there was a God.

At age seventeen, I couldn't take it anymore. I said goodbye to my parents and headed to a refugee camp just inside

Thailand. My trip took two weeks because I often hid; I didn't have a passport. It was scary, including the last part where the Thai military patrolled the river border; they didn't want us. Finally, I arrived at a camp and lived there for six years. I finished high school, including Bible classes. I learned about God, but I didn't really know Him.

At age twenty-three, I gained a refugee visa, borrowed $1004 from USCIS (United States Citizenship and Immigration Services) for the plane ticket, and flew to Nebraska, USA. I had no money and only a small bag of personal things. I didn't know what would happen, but I prayed and God made me strong. I soon met a sweet man, Lay Klek, got married, and moved to Atlanta.

USA life is hard because people are so busy. I didn't know English nor did I know anyone here, except my husband who always works the second shift. After our second son was born here, I was with the children all day . . . every day. I was very tired. I couldn't go back to my job for six months. My pregnancy with my third son was the most difficult. When it was time to deliver at the hospital, it seemed like I was dying, and I panicked. I was "walking through the valley of the shadow of death" as in Psalm 23:4. But suddenly I wasn't afraid. God was with me. It felt like He was standing at my side. Then my baby was born through a C-section. I realized then that Jesus Christ had been helping me my whole life.

Covid-19 suddenly hit our community. I began to contrast that invisible disease with the invisible God. I knew that God was stronger and began to earnestly study the Bible with my American friend, Mary. Studying God's Word always gives me strength. Jesus Christ came to show us what God is like, and to save us. John 1:12 says, "To all who received Him, He gave the right to become the children of God." I believe this.

Since coming to Jesus Christ, I now understand why the Burmese military has tried to annihilate my people for more than seventy years. I understand why the military has bombed schools and machine-gunned teachers. I understand why government soldiers burned down my home and destroyed my village. It's because they do not know or love Jesus Christ.

When my kids are grown, I will return to Myanmar to tell the Burmese military about the love of Jesus Christ. Maybe this is God's plan for me, to be like John who baptized many people. YES, this is God's purpose for me that I be His messenger, wherever I am!

Elic

Elic is now a joyful follower of Christ. When you ask her "What do you like best about America?" she says: "I like everything." She loves the freedom, safety, and opportunity that America offers. She and her husband, Lay Klek, have three healthy sons, ages nine, six, and three. She's a soccer mom, Sunday School teacher, and translator for many of the ethnic Karen activities, including a weekly Bible study in Clarkston. She wants to return to Myanmar someday to be a missionary to the Burmese military. Her favorite Scripture is Proverbs 31:10 that says, "Who can find a virtuous woman? For her price is far above rubies." Adoniram Judson, America's first missionary to Burma in 1812, would be so proud to meet her.

5

✝ *A Rapper's Tragedy and Triumph*

▼

by Adrian Moore

January 2008 found me broken and frozen; totally my fault. I was a narcissist. As I pulled into the driveway, I saw my wife sitting on the front steps of our house. We had fought the night before, like we had done so often in our twelve years of marriage. But last night was different, and the look on her face was proof enough. She was the first and only woman that I ever truly loved. I had married her and had loved her with all of the love that I knew.

We walked into the house and called my eleven-year-old daughter and my nine-year-old son into the room. I couldn't look at their faces. My wife spoke. "Mommy and Daddy are getting a divorce." I don't know of any pain worse than watching your children fall apart in front of your face, knowing it's totally your fault, and knowing you can't fix it with a hug.

I walked out to my car. As I turned the ignition, I glanced into the rearview mirror. I saw myself: evil looking back at me. I suddenly realized that I was the problem. I had just crossed a line, a point of no return. I didn't believe in what the Bible describes as hell, but I deserved it and dreaded it.

Six years later in 2014, I got a call from my best friend. He always had time for me. He never judged me. He was strong, wise, patient, sharp, clean and noble, everything I wanted to be. As the phone call neared its end, he said, "By the way, I'm a Christian now."

"Why?!" I blurted out. The best person I knew was telling me the most ridiculous thing I could possibly hear. I had to at least think about it.

To appreciate my shock, you must understand how much I idolized this man. I believed that he knew secret things about the universe, God, and other things. I had been following as his student in a practice he had called "The Way." I thought I was on a mystical journey to unlocking the power of God within, including Jesus. But "God in flesh" was a phrase for delusional Christians.

Two days later (July 5), I called him back, saying, "So, you mean Jesus is your Lord and Savior and all that crap?" "Yup," he said. "Christians aren't the fools, but I am?" "Yup," he said again. I couldn't argue anymore. I walked out the back door of my house and stared up at the night sky. "Lord Jesus," I prayed, "please come and heal my darkness." The next moment was the most wonderful experience of my life. I saw and felt something, and I heard His voice in my heart. I received Jesus Christ and instantly knew that He is real, that He is alive, and that He is God. He said: "I have always had you; now follow Me."

I cried more deeply and purely than I ever had or would. I cried because Jesus had shown Himself, His beauty, His goodness, and His glory…to me. I cried because I saw that all my sins were against Him, the most holy, the most innocent, and the One who loved me. I cried because He had forgiven me, and I knew that He would never throw me away. In these eight years I have had failures and forgiveness, peace, and rescue from sin. I have never stopped shedding tears of thankfulness.

Two years later, I worked as a chauffeur, and sometimes drove limousines. One day I had a stretch of time with a few hours to kill. As I ate lunch, I made a witnessing plan to rap. I had rapped before, even for total strangers. Today would be different. My goal was to rap at 38th and Michigan Ave. It's a needy area: dealers, thugs, gang members, homeless people, and people really struggling. They need Jesus, and I was determined to share the Good News. I wasn't afraid of getting robbed or hurt; I was only afraid that I would back down.

A group of young guys stood near a corner grocery store. They noticed me right away: a shiny black limo with me in a black suit with black shades. So, I, this pasty white guy, yelled out, "Who wants to rap battle?" Instantly, I was the most entertaining thing around, and I hadn't even started yet. They were laughing and jostling with each other.

One of the guys stepped up and said he'd battle rap me. I told him he'd better go first, because he wouldn't want to go after I was done. His friends were egging him on. He told me to go first, so I hit the limo's sound system and did three songs. My opponent didn't want to rap after that. They gave me props and fist-bumps, and I told them to think about

Jesus. As I drove away, I was thanking God that He had given me the courage to share His love.

When I first started writing rap songs, they were about Jesus, but also it was about showing off my talent and creativity. Over these last eight years, I've made it about Him.

Since 2019, I've been on staff at Mount Carmel Elementary School near Jackson, Kentucky. This is a great privilege for me. The old me is dead. There is a new me, a loving me, one that lives for God. Yet not me but Christ in me. By God's grace, I love the truth of 2 Corinthians 5:17 that says, "Therefore, if anyone is in Christ, the new creation has come: The old has gone, the new is here!" and Galatians 2:20-21 that says,

> *I have been crucified with Christ and I no longer live, but Christ lives in me. The life I now live in the body, I live by faith in the Son of God, who loved me and gave himself for me. I do not set aside the grace of God, for if righteousness could be gained through the law, Christ died for nothing!*

Adrian Moore

Adrian's greatest treasures are his two children: Ivy (26) and William (24). He says, "My kids grew up so fast—so much life, so much potential, so much pain. I pray about them every day and am trusting our heavenly Father to do beautiful things in their lives."

Adrian loves to share Jesus. Prior to hearing about CWC, he shared his conversion story many times, but writing it down for this *Jesus Can* book has provided fresh healing for him. It took him back in a special way to that wonderful moment when Christ came to him.

6

◎ ✝ *Love Conquers Fear*

▼

by Jane Jackson

As far back as I can remember, I believed in God. We were a religious family, attended church regularly, and prayed together. I was shy growing up and often felt very insecure.

When I was a junior in high school, I met with the guidance counselor to discuss my future plans. I didn't have direction on what to do after high school. I finally decided to become a registered nurse. The counselor didn't think I would make it because science classes were hard for me. I went forward with it anyway and succeeded!

I got a job working at a local hospital in OB, Labor, and Delivery. Two weeks after graduation, I remember thinking, "Everything is going so well in my life! I love my job, I'm dating a man I hope to marry, etc., but why do I feel so empty inside?" Shortly after that, I discovered my boyfriend was dating someone else. My world came crashing down.

I didn't care about my job, couldn't eat or sleep, and nothing mattered. It was during this dark time in my life that I received a letter from my brother, Bob. He told me he loved me very much, but his heart was heavy for me, and he feared I was a lost girl, headed for a lost eternity. I nearly tore up the letter! But what he wrote next was, "I love you so much that I would be willing to die in your place if that would help you come to know Jesus."

That's when God touched my heart and opened my eyes to see that Jesus had already died for me on the Cross nearly 2000 years ago. I got down on my knees, and I asked Jesus to forgive my sins and come into my heart to be my Savior and Lord. Depression and fear were lifted, replaced by peace and joy that settled into my soul. John 3:16 became personal to me. "For God so loved the world that He gave His only Son, that whoever believes in Him will not perish, but have eternal life." The facts that I had learned about God when I was a child became reality in my heart, and I had a personal relationship with a living, loving God!

I used to fear death. What if I didn't do enough good things to get into heaven? Nobody can know for sure, right? Wrong! I learned that the Bible says in Ephesians 2: 8-9, "It is by grace you have been saved, through faith, this is not from yourselves, it is the gift of God." I realized that Jesus finished the work needed to save me and all who humbly come to Him in faith and repentance. First John 5:13 talks about those who believe in the name of the Son of God, that they may know that they have eternal life. To know for sure that my sins were forgiven and God had a place for me in heaven was a huge relief and joy to me.

Before that point in my life, I had a lot of fear and insecurities—fear about what people thought of me, fear of making mistakes, or fear of being rejected circled in my mind. Then I discovered and believed 1 John 4:18, "There is no fear in love. But perfect love casts out fear." I prayed, "God, if that is true, then make it real in my life." And He did, giving me His love that conquers fears and helping me to reach out to others.

I told the Lord I wanted to live for Him and let Him lead my life. For example, I stopped looking for a husband. I'd leave that up to God. I started attending a Bible teaching church, and a month later I met a man (named Bob) who became my husband a year later. We both loved singing and sharing our faith in Jesus, and we formed a band called "Friends." A few years after our marriage, we had a son, Thomas, whose name means "twin or double blessing." We were overjoyed! God was giving us the desires of our hearts.

We told the Lord we would be willing to go wherever He wanted us to go and do whatever He wanted us to do. Little did we know that He would lead us down the jungle paths of Irian Jaya, Indonesia. I worked at the mission hospital. My husband did repairs at the hospital and missionary homes, and he helped at the hospital when we needed him. We homeschooled our son, and we also shared Jesus' love with the village people through our music.

There had been a doctor and three nurses at the hospital before we arrived, but during our time there, just one other nurse, Gail, was there and no doctor. Worse, Gail flew out to the coast for a week, so I was alone. I delivered babies, gave medication, cleaned wounds, treated burns, and did whatever was needed. A patient was brought to the hospital badly needing stitches. I wasn't trained for that! I wanted to run away, but where could I go? I was in the jungle! The ends of the earth! It was hot and humid, and I was scared. My glasses steamed up, and I thought I was going to faint. I prayed. God answered. I put the stitches in as best as I could. God used the weak (me) to show His strength. A dying boy was also brought in. I tried everything. Nothing was helping. We cried out to God. He heard and healed the little boy.

The next week, when Gail was back, a hunter was carried in. His friends had paddled their canoe for two weeks to bring him. He had been gored and bitten by a wild boar. His wounds were badly infected. His right kneecap had been torn back, and he had large gouges of flesh bitten out of his back and leg. The horrible smell from rotting flesh was overpowering. I prayed a quick prayer, "God, are you sure you have the right nurse here because I don't know if I can do this?" As we cleaned deeper in the wounds, maggots came crawling out! Gag! Later I learned that maggots help to clean wounds. You've heard of natural medicine? Oh, and did I tell you I'm afraid of bugs too? God was/is with me. Immanuel.

After six months in Irian Jaya, God led us to work at the Christian Academy in Tokyo, Japan. I was the school nurse, and my husband taught Industrial Arts. We had many opportunities to share Jesus' love, and also had many opportunities to do concerts in English and Japanese. Our son loved the school, made many friends, and grew in his faith. We grew as a family.

We served in Japan for four-and-a-half years, then returned home to Wisconsin. My father was terminally ill. Three days after our return, he prayed to receive Jesus into his heart. It was beautiful to see peace in Dad's life. He lived another eighteen months. Shortly before he died, I asked him if there was anything he wanted to say to my brothers and sisters. Without hesitation he said, "Know Jesus, love Jesus, and tell as many people about Him as you can." His last words were, "Saving grace. Saving grace."

With God, nothing is impossible. He has a plan for each of us, and it's good. Jeremiah 29:11 states,

> *"For I know the plans I have for you," declares the LORD, "plans to prosper you and not to harm you, plans to give you hope and a future."*

Jane Jackson

Jane loves being a Christian, wife, mom, grandma, friend, nurse and musician. She's worked stateside and overseas as an RN in obstetrics, pediatrics, jungle nursing, school nursing, hospice, public health, and mental health/ behavioral health.

7

✝ *The Everlasting Impact of Billy Graham*

▼

by Kenyon Ross

As a son of a pastor, and brother of two pastors, I watched every move my parents made, especially my father. I watched him rise early to study God's Word, and I watched how God moved his heart to tears whenever the Spirit led.

No one could capture the attention of a congregation like my father. "Welcome! Welcome to a church of sinners. Sinners saved by grace" is how he opened the service every Sunday.

He was such a good dad and had great friends. As a teen, Dad lived near Rev. Billy Graham's family in North Carolina and became close friends with the Graham kids. In casual conversation, Dad told Rev. Graham of his plans to enroll in Samford University (Birmingham, Alabama) in the Fall of 1960. As it turns out, twenty years prior, Billy had an evangelist friend named Harold Johnson, whose daughter Haroldine "Deedie" Johnson would also be enrolling at Samford in the

Fall of 1960. Sadly, Harold died when Deedie was a young girl, so she didn't have the funds to finish schooling. But Rev. Graham took care of all those bills and urged my dad to look for Deedie on campus. She was already engaged, but that soon changed because of my dad's magnetic Ross DNA. They soon fell in love, were married, and had kids, including me!

I have a godly heritage. By the time I was eight, I heard the Bible message multiple times around the dinner table. Just like in the pulpit, my dad and the Holy Spirit brought Truth to daily life. In 1978 the men of our church did a retreat down the Swanee River in Florida. My dad and I were canoeing along the riverbank when a poisonous snake dropped out of an overhanging tree and, just missing us, fell into the river. That shook me up. What if it had fallen into our boat, bit me, and…. I didn't know where I would go if I had died that day.

On the way home I asked my dad about the Ten Commandments. Arriving home, I went into our guest room and prayed for three hours. I reflected on the commandments, understood that I couldn't keep them perfectly, and asked God into my heart. At eight, I likely hadn't done anything too terrible, but I knew I was fallen without God. It was an immediate transformation in my heart. From that day, God has been working on me, helping me understand what it means to be His heir. In my teen years, I sometimes found myself wandering away. I remember having a good cry once every two to three months, which was good for my soul. The Lord was bringing me back.

After high school I enrolled at my parents' alma mater,

Samford University. I regularly attended a campus ministry and also a summer project in Florida: 150 collegians, plus chaperones, packed into a motel. We learned to walk with the Lord and to tell others about Him. One of those 150 students was a young lady I had met earlier that year, Ami Phillips. After a long and healthy courtship, I proposed and thankfully she accepted. It's been an exciting life together. Our sweetest treasures are our grown children: Jackson (25), Katie (22), and Izzy (18), all living near us in Birmingham, Alabama. The frosting on the cake is that Ami and I just celebrated our wedding anniversary in March. After thirty plus years, she's holding up remarkably well!

Ami and I have been active at Shades Valley Community Church for the past twenty-five years. Initially I was busy for ten years in the men's ministry. Then God led me to go door-to-door in our church's neighborhood, visiting over 600 homes on Wednesday nights. I was privileged to share Christ and pray with many people.

One night, since it had poured rain all day, I wanted to stay home. But I negotiated with God, saying, "I'll go to the streets if You stop the rain." So, I drove to the first home in the pouring rain and prayed, "OK God, I'm here. I'm going to open my car door. If you make it stop raining, I'll walk to this first house." I opened my door and the rain stopped. You know, sometimes you can hear a big rain coming. Well, I saw and heard it leave. I went to eight consecutive houses, sharing invitations to church, and I never felt a drop of rain. Every time I stepped under a home's porch or awning, the rain would pour behind me but never touch me. On the second to last house, I was speaking with a little old lady on her covered porch, and just for fun I said, "Watch this." I stepped out from under her porch roof, thinking God would stop the rain, just for me, at that very moment, just like He had at the last eight homes. He didn't . . . (sigh). I was a little overconfident and got soaked. I had one more home to visit. Even though I was drenched, I forced myself to knock on that door. The guy had no problem with me being sopping wet, and our conversation was the closest I came to leading someone to Christ that night . . . nine steps ahead . . . one step back.

Kenyon Ross

Among other creative ways to love their neighbors, Kenyon and his friends at SVC church launched a Farmers Market fourteen years ago with ten booths, including baked goods, craft booths, food trucks, live entertainment, and kids' activities. This 2024 season was the fourteenth and hosted seventy vendors every Tuesday night. Literally thousands of west Homewood, Alabama neighbors attend during the summer months (www.westhomewood.com). The market was voted the #1 Farmers Market in Central Alabama by AL.com readers. Kenyon has given many interviews to use this venue to share the love of Christ.

8

Loving the Little People

by Samantha Gilson

I have always believed that our purpose as Christians while we are here on earth is to spread the love and Word of Jesus to as many people as possible. Accomplishing that goal looks very different for each individual person. Some people find purpose in their job, in doing their work well, or in spreading joy and love in their workplace. Others find purpose in service: giving their time, love, money, or other means is how they best show God's love to the world. Even the spreading of God's love and Word can look different. Sometimes you plant a seed, like as a teacher, when you can't necessarily vocalize why you are more positive, loving, or patient than your peers, but the kids know. Sometimes it is more overt, like sharing the gospel with a friend or family member. But most of the time it seems to fall somewhere in between, like praying with a stranger, or saying "God Bless You" when someone sneezes. The important thing seems to be listening to the nudging of the Holy Spirit inside you to let you know which step is yours to take, and what needs to be left to someone else.

I have found my purpose in loving the little children in my life. I have found that with my daughter, son, nieces, and other children I encounter through church or in the community, I can speak more freely than I can in my capacity as a teacher. I get to show them love and speak about God more overtly! I can prompt conversations about baptism and salvation. It has been very freeing to have more time with them.

When I had my daughter, I was still teaching in a traditional school. I felt a pull for a while, but much stronger while on maternity leave, to search for an online position. God opened doors for me to work online, teaching from home. I teach math and science and absolutely love my work. I enjoyed being a teacher but always felt constricted by the time and regulations placed on traditional learning. I truly believe each learner should be treated as an individual, free to move at their own pace and learn in their own way. Traditional education never allowed for that flexibility in timing for sure, and rarely in method of learning. I also remember feeling so drained at the end of each day from the discipline and classroom management that was necessary when I had thirty fifteen year olds in a classroom three times a day for an hour and a half apiece. I never felt like I got to do as much teaching, and definitely not as much individualized learning as I would have liked since I was just trying to survive each day.

Now as I am teaching online, I still am able to speak with students, but instead of having to be the disciplinarian I get to be concerned, take interest in their lives, show more love and compassion than I ever had time to do in the traditional setting. I also get to help them exactly where they are and in the way that they need. I don't have to teach the median of the thirty students, I can help one or two with a particular assignment and then another with something completely different. I can differentiate based on learning styles and special needs. I can consider what is going on in their lives and show them the love and compassion of Christ in an individualized and meaningful way. And best of all, I have gotten to see every big step in my daughter's and son's lives. I have gotten to be a part of helping them to learn and grow. I can be home for my nieces to provide a safe space after school each day for them to decompress, be kids, and get any extra educational help that they may need as they learn to be good humans and good Christians.

I have always tried to follow God's plan for my life, and some days that just felt like surviving my current battle. But since His plan has been more fully implemented, I have felt more freedom to live my purpose and show His love, patience, kindness, compassion, and guidance to all the little people in my life. I would encourage you to spend some time with Him each day and ask earnestly that He reveal your next best step, that He open your eyes to your purpose, and that He prepare your heart and mind to fulfill that purpose whatever it may be. Be warned—it might surprise you when you find out what it is!

Samantha Gilson

Samantha is a math/chemistry teacher and cheer/dance coach from Kentucky. She currently lives in Alabama with her husband, daughter, son, dogs, and cat. In her free time (which is not much with two children), you will find her reading, in the sun, or swimming. Samantha joined the CWC to share the stories of God working in her life in hopes that they may help/inspire others as they demonstrate His love and grand plan.

9

✝ *Left for Dead, but Now Alive Forevermore*

▼

by Isaiah

I was born in Africa. Where we're from is vital, but where we're going is immortal. And contrary to shallow thinking, success is not determined by who you know, or who you are, but *whose* you are.

One of the perks of belonging to the Lover of our Souls is instant siblings—we're able to meet total strangers and feel total acceptance. A few months ago, I was privileged to meet Stephanie, CWC's founder, and fellowship with other beautiful people like Martha, Pastor Marc, Nancy, Vermon, and Todd. I am a truly rich man.

At age seven, my devoted dad took me to church. Of all the fathers on the planet, Dad gave me the chance that many kids only dream of—meeting with God's people, imperfect as we are, in His house. We worshiped the King in that frail building where I was born again. He *chose* me. By the way, if you haven't already done so, please watch *The Chosen* with an open heart. Eternity will show its lasting results.

I faced many dangers growing up, and many challenges to my faith; it wavered, but He didn't. I came back to Christ when I was twenty-two, grew in grace and truth, and was chosen as a church elder. My homeland was experiencing a gut-wrenching, and literally gut-cutting, war in those days. I served as a government infantryman for nine years. Some films about that era are accurate but skim the surface of how dirtbag demons can utterly control naïve humans. These are nightmarish memories, so I will describe them only briefly.

While serving at my military post, an enemy sniper shot me in the chest, and I was taken to a clinic. My wound was so bloodied that the nurses considered me half dead already, so I was left untreated. As an RN later told me, when they saw that I was still alive the next morning, they did ER surgery to remove the AK-47 bullet from my chest. I spent the next three months there, and the doctor said it would be impossible for me to ever lift anything heavy. You know, the Almighty loves to hear those wimpy words. He healed me. I've been doing construction work in America for over twenty years and am as strong as an ox, in my humble opinion of course.

My friend Jeremiah was a world class soccer player in those days and was well known. When the rebels captured him, they were hoping to recruit him. They wanted him to burn down homes and schools, but he cursed at them. That same hour they cut off his forearms with a dull machete. He passed out, lost a lot of blood, and was left for dead. About an hour later, a friend of mine found him, put him in a wheelbarrow, and pushed him half a mile to a peacekeeping clinic which became his home for seven months. Because the heartless war for priceless gems was still ongoing, Jeremiah and I escaped by boat to neighboring Guinea. We applied for refugee visas to America and were granted them a year later. We boarded the plane with no money, no luggage, no change of clothes, and no carry-on except for my Bible. It was enough.

Shortly after arriving, we were wonderfully loved by God's people who arranged employment for me, which provided steady work for nine years and many chances to share Christ. Then that job ended. God was calling me to do evangelism full time, so I opted for an early severance check. I used it to buy many musical instruments for worship in a new church that we started.

In 1997, I married God's finest woman for me. By glorious grace, she bore us two sons. We almost lost the older son to sickle cell disease when he was ten years old. Thankfully, his younger brother was happy to be his brother's keeper by sharing bone marrow with him that brought healing.

My favorite verse is Psalm 16:11.

>To God be the glory through Jesus Christ our Savior.

Isaiah

Having been shot by an AK-47, Isaiah was left for dead on the clinic floor. Just before passing out, he vowed to live wholly for the Lord if his life was spared. That was 1992 in Sierra Leone, and Isaiah has kept his promise. He's the founding pastor of His Right Hand Ministries International on Milwaukee's northside and loves to share the Gospel anywhere, anytime. Isaiah is requesting prayer for his younger brother, a double amputee, who loves the Lord but is struggling to overcome the trauma of war.

10

Living in the Shadow

by Kim Patterson

All my life I've felt like I've lived under someone else's shadow, not being the best and not being seen. I strived to be the best in everything I did. I tried to get noticed and do things that would put me in the spotlight. But there was always someone else outshining me. Even if I was the best at something, it felt like an accident. Never did I feel like I was the best. I would think, *There must be some mistake. This can't be right.*

In the seventh grade, my first year as a cheerleader, I was chosen to be the captain. I was shy and quiet, and I didn't see myself as a captain. What did everyone else see that I didn't? I ended up being the captain four out of the six years I cheered. As a cheerleader, your main job is to cheer and encourage others, motivate them to do their best, and help change the atmosphere of discouragement into hopefulness for victory. Even as a cheerleader, I existed to help someone else reach their full potential. I was not the star; they were.

And, I was the best at it. I was the best at living under the shadow of someone else.

Around this same time, I was also on the softball team. I was really good but nowhere near the best. It seemed I was in the shadow of this other player. In fact, I was positioned to help make her shine. She was the lead off batter and always got on base. Then I was up next. I too would always get on base, but not until I gave her an opportunity to steal second then third base. You see, she was fast. When I would hit the ball, no one cared that I made it to first base and sometimes second, because they were all watching and cheering as she ran across home plate. My job was to run around those bases following as her shadow.

As an adult, I went to work with my mom's company. She was a superstar in there. She rose to the top quickly and gave motivational talks to not only the people who worked underneath her but to the entire company. She brought me under her wing and taught me everything she knew. I began to do well and moved up. But I was always introduced as her daughter, not really having an identity of my own. No matter how well I did, I couldn't get out from under her shadow because she was so big.

Mine has been a life spent in the shadows. Oh the blessing of being trained under the Shadow! Look what Psalm 91 has to say about life in the Shadow. "Those who dwell in the shelter of the Most High will find rest in the Shadow of the Almighty." Not only does it provide rest but also protection. Many people find it difficult to come underneath His Shadow because they long for their lives to have meaningful purpose. The lie is that if you're not doing something big, then maybe that makes you insignificant. Believe me, I know. But having been trained under the shadow of others helped me value the benefits of dwelling in that shadow. It's in the shadow that I learned my true purpose and found my significance.

As a cheerleader, I learned the purpose of encouraging others. "And let us consider how we may spur one another on toward love and good deeds, not giving up meeting together as some are in the habit of doing, as encouraging one another" (Hebrews 3:13). Also, it helped me understand and value others above myself. "Do not think of yourself more highly than you ought" (Romans 12:3). From softball, I learned that my significance is found in following the One who goes before me, guiding me, leading and clearing the way for me, removing any obstacles or hinderances, remembering that "I must decrease, so that He can increase" (John 3:30).

Finally, my significance comes from being the daughter of the Most High God. Because He is my Father, everything He has is mine (Luke 15:31). Every resource is available to me. Every promise is kept. Every need is supplied, and every gift is good. And He is taking me under His wing, and I reflect His glory when I allow Him to conform me to the image of Christ. This is what is learned from a life lived in the shadow—humility. "For those who exalt themselves will be humbled, and those who humble themselves will be exalted" (Luke 14:11). My Father sees me under His shadow, and it is there that I not only find my rest and protection, but my significance as "I shine like a star in the universe" (Philippians 2:15).

In the book of Acts, we're told that many brought the sick out into the streets so that when Peter walked by, his shadow might fall on them and heal them (Acts 5:15). Did Peter's shadow have the power to heal people? No, certainly not! But, the One who overshadowed Peter did. God has the power to do healing work in people's lives, and when we live and work underneath His shadow, God can use us for His purposes. People are saved when they hear the gospel, comforted when shown compassion, and find peace when they feel loved. And yes, there is healing for your body when God's wings stretch over you. "The Sun of Righteousness rises with healing in His wings" (Malachi 4:2).

Your life has great purpose when you can dwell underneath the Shadow of the Most High. God can use you to impact the lives of others. When you can be content living hidden, like a jewel waiting to shine when the light hits it, is when your life becomes the most beautiful. Oh, to be one of His precious gems within His treasure chest, shining with all the facets of His likeness. Your life can leave behind a legacy of love, kindness, healing, and restoration.

I spent most of my life going on what I'd call a treasure hunt, trying to find what I was good at, what made me special, and how I could stand out. I couldn't discover this while under the shadow of others, but once I got under God's Shadow, I began to realize that I was one of those treasures. God sees me as one of His gems, valuable and beautiful. I am a diamond that He sets in the sky to shine brightly for Him. Discovering a life of purpose begins when you realize you are significant to God.

It occurred to me one day when I was thinking about a lost

diamond, which God had once helped me find, that He was now helping me find myself. In finding the diamond, God revealed Himself and that was the beginning of revealing me. You see, I was the diamond who was lost. And He is the one who searches for the lost and brings them out of hiding. Knowing God loved me enough to help me find my diamond put me on a search to know Him more. To know the God who cared enough to reach down into my world and reveal Himself was the start of my treasure hunt. Little did I know, the treasure He wanted me to find was me. In finding Him, I found myself. My true self. The more of God I was looking for was found within me! And there is so much more to me, but I've learned that more can only be found living in His Shadow. . . on purpose.

Kim Patterson

Kim Patterson is a wife and mother of three. She has been a leader in her church for the past fourteen years, leading various small groups and teaching Bible studies. Kim has a passion for women's ministries and discipleship. It is her love for the Lord that fuels her desire to see others grow in Christ and walk in freedom and victory.

11

✝ *Loved with An Everlasting Love*

▼

by Linda Holmes

Hi friends! I'm a lover of Jesus, housewife, mom of three boys, and business owner. I grew up in a rural town in south Alabama, the Bible Belt. I am the youngest of four sisters and favorite of my parents...ha!

I grew up in an upbeat household. My parents are God-fearing and hard workers, so my sisters and I had a very good childhood. We grew up going to church, not every Sunday but on the ones that we thought mattered the most. I had a reverence for God but lived most of my child/teen/young adult years for myself. I didn't think much about it because all of my friends lived the same way. When you hang with people that always agree with you, it's easy to feel fine whatever you're doing.

I drank a lot, no big deal. I could handle my liquor. True or false? You know the answer. I dated around. Finally, I began to view life differently so I thought maybe I should go to church. I went on and off when I needed to feel good. A word to the wise: If a church always makes you feel good about you and your secret sins, get out while you can.

Eventually I started dating a wonderful man named Scott. By God's glorious grace, we married and it's going on twenty-five years that we have been together! In that first year of marriage, I felt so drawn to stop drinking and go to church. It was God working in me. One night I prayed with many tears that if God was real, to please save me and give me the peace I had been hearing and reading about in the Bible. I hadn't studied the Bible but would pick it up sometimes when I was feeling really down.

Scott and I moved back to my hometown so I started going to a small church there. I went alone. God hadn't worked on my husband yet. (I thank God for working in Scott's life soon after that.) God was drawing me to Himself, which was wonderful. I stopped drinking and started hanging out with Christians who helped me so much. I began experiencing the reality of the peace with God that comes when you stop trying to impress God and trust in Jesus Christ alone to save you from sin, now and forever as described in Romans 5:1. I also experienced the peace of God which is a day-to-day thing. Sadly, I still sin . . . (groan). I'm far from perfect. But the Savior promises that when we confess our sin, He forgives us and cleanses us from those toxic thoughts, words, or actions as it says in 1 John 1:9 and Philippians 4:6-8.

One day I was asked to tell my testimony to a group of people. I thought, *I don't have a very dramatic one.* I mean, I wasn't enslaved in the total wasted world of SAD: sex, alcoholism, and drugs. It was then that I fully realized the Lord saved me. He saved me from a gradually self-destructive lifestyle of zero purpose, zero hope, zero future. He also spared me from a forever, endless eternity without love, friends, joy, peace, safety, grace and truth, in a word, hell. So I realized that every person that Jesus Christ saves has a testimony, from darkness to light, from fear to courage, from death to life. He gives us His Spirit, righteousness, wisdom, love, beauty, purity, all that is heavenly…in exchange for our ashes.

How about you, dear friend? May I introduce you to the Lover of your soul?

As parents, we mess up a lot. On some days, it's nonstop and downright embarrassing. We love our children more than words can say, but we too are sinners and disappoint them. Thankfully, our good, good Father in heaven isn't like that. We trust Him because He is totally trustworthy.

If you're not a follower of Jesus Christ, I pray you will seek Him. He has done incredibly beautiful things for thousands of years and for millions of people, including me. IF you seek Him with your whole heart, you too can find Him. Jesus is the only way! I pray Heaven's best blessings to you.

Linda Holmes

Linda and her husband, Scott, enjoy sharing the Word of God as they mentor and teach the College and Career Sunday School class at their church in Monroeville, Alabama. Linda is a supermom of three guys and teaches 4th-6th grade young people on Wednesday nights. She has served with Save-a-Life which has benefitted many people, especially teen girls, in their community for many years. Among all the eternal promises of God, her favorite is John 3:16. There's so much love there.

12

✝ *From Cambodia's Killing Fields to Alabama's Lumberyards and Back*

▼

by Long Kuoy

I was born in Cambodia in 1947. My parents were Buddhist. We never knew peace, personally or nationally. For example, socialist Pol Pot demanded "equity." Forty-five months later, three million people were "equally" dead. Mere words can't describe the horrors.

My homeland is infamous for Khmer Rouge socialism. The KR were political activists and prided themselves in the murder of two million people, including my two brothers who disappeared. The KR utopian dream demanded nightmarish murders, whether teachers at schools or workers on their farms, which became known as the Killing Fields. An additional one million people, including my father, died of starvation and disease; the KR prevented access to medicine which could have saved thousands of lives.

Jesus Can...

At 24, I married my sweetheart, Seakleng, on May 25, 1971. She bore our first child a year later. Our second child was born in 1974. At that time, the KR began forcing everyone to work in the rice fields. Anyone who wouldn't or couldn't do so was tortured and left to die. The KR targeted businessmen, community leaders, and artists. To be literate was a death sentence.

After a few years under KR socialism, some Cambodians escaped to the Thai border. Finally, in 1979, the Red Cross and other groups built a large camp for Cambodian refugees just inside Thailand. My wife, three daughters, and I escaped and took shelter in that camp. We gained safety but not freedom. We couldn't leave the camp nor seek employment. We were given enough water and rice to survive and sometimes dry fish or beans. We were certainly thankful for all of those, but we yearned for freedom and peace, if they existed at all.

In that refugee camp, some Cambodians made a Buddhist altar. I never went there as I had been Buddhist for thirty plus years, but was still "lost." Providentially, the UN built a small church facility there. About the same time, I came across a gospel tract that reminded me of how dangerous life is. Finally, I began to read the Bible, which offered true salvation through the Prince of Peace. Those words fed my starving soul.

After three months of Bible study and prayer with those new friends, I fully understood the gospel. Jesus received the death penalty for me...dying on the cross for me. He allowed people to crucify Him. He is God, so it was easy for Him to come back to life after being dead for three days. So, I

Give You Purpose

humbly repented of my sin and gladly received Jesus into my life. Then I was baptized as a witness to the world. I became a new person, living with hope now and forever.

You know, the average waiting time for an international refugee to get a visa to another country is seventeen years. For my wife and three girls and me, it was two years. That was still very long for us, but it could have been much worse. In 1981, we got visas to America and arrived on Dec. 18. Mobile, Alabama, was our first home. Our sponsor was very helpful in many ways, especially in getting medical attention for my wife. An Xray found a tuberculosis spot on her lung, but they couldn't treat it because she was six months pregnant. Then John was born. By that time, half of one of her lungs had tuberculosis. By God's grace, she received successful treatment for that. We are very thankful for dear medical workers and excellent medical treatment in America.

In 1982 we moved to Monroeville, Alabama, where I worked in the lumber industry. My supervisors and coworkers were always very kind to me. I've been warmly welcomed in sweet home Alabama! To spend more time with my family and in ministry, I took an early retirement in 2009 at age 62½. Rev. Micah Gandy began pastoring in Monroeville that same year and has blessed our family by his excellent Bible teaching; he is the best. He arranged for me to make mission trips to Trinidad and also inspired us to prepare 200 shoe boxes annually to send to needy children as part of Samaritan's Purse outreach.

I am thankful for our church here that enabled me to make annual mission trips to Cambodia, beginning in 2009. In January 2023, my trip was for one month joining 100th anniversary celebrations, thanking God for the many lives that have been changed by the gospel, which came to Cambodia in 1923. I was amazed by the thousands of people at the celebrations, including many American and European missionaries. They spoke Cambodian fluently, which brought me to tears. Despite being foreigners, they have given their lives to serve Cambodians. These large meetings took place in the former killing fields, which are now living fields and productive farms. One of the purposes for the January celebrations was to reach out to the new generation of young people, many of whom are naïve about the violence of KR and 21st century sophisticated atheism. One of the speakers quoted Pastor Chheak Tang, who was murdered by the KR in 1977. Tang had written, "If I weep, I weep because my people do not know Christ." January's speaker also quoted a portion of Pastor Tang's favorite hymn, "Jesus, hold my hand as I keep running this race. O Jesus, help us to have victory."

A sad memory of my January trip was visiting a museum that contained many drawings of where and how the KR had tortured many people during those forty-five months in the 1970s. I went there because it's part of my heritage. Three million died in those months of unimaginable suffering and torture. I am no better than they are, and I weep for them. Yet God spared me, and I weep with thanksgiving for the Cross.

Long Kuoy

Long Kuoy enjoys gardening and watching life spring up! Similarly, he loves sowing seeds of the Gospel and nurturing spiritual growth in people's lives. He also enjoys fixing machines, which always reminds him of his broken life in Cambodia, and God's faithfulness to restore and give him a new life. Long and Seakleng have four children, six grands, and one great grand.

13

† *No Longer a Lost Cause*

▼

by Ronnie Blanton

I rebelled against my parents, school teachers, and the legal system. I embraced the philosophy of "live for today." In fact, there was a song with those words that echoed in my head. All of this led to a lifestyle of partying, drugs, and alcohol. I was my own boundary setter if there were any. Along with some running buddies, I never kept my promise to do right. I don't know how my wife put up with me as long as she did. After eight years, she finally filed for divorce. Life was all about me and what I wanted; I never worried about others and how they were getting hurt.

My parents were always trying to help me. They experienced a lot of suffering because of me. They wanted to retire so they sold their established business, the Tally Ho Café, to my younger brother, my wife, and me. It was a good chance for me to make a genuine contribution to the community. Instead, I got into motorcycles. But riding was not just to ride. We rode together, drank, and smoked weed every weekend and anytime we got the chance. When my family confronted me with my lost ways, I loaded my bike and hit the road, running from my problems.

After losing my family and business, my job in those days was building a logging road in the woods. After lunch one day, we got high and I got the truck stuck. We tried to free it but warped the frame and basically destroyed the truck. I lost my job, my money, and was soon living in a 16 ft by 16 ft shack that I made from used lumber. I spent the next two weeks drinking. I was extremely depressed. But my dad came by and offered me a chance to make some money as a carpenter if I'd join a mission trip to Kentucky. I told him I'd go, but if anybody started preaching to me I would catch a bus home. Looking back, God was working in ways I knew nothing about.

We traveled 600+ miles one way to Pippa Pass in Kentucky's poorest county. I was on the grungy side with hair down to my waist, but my traveling companions didn't mind. We all enjoyed the trip without tripping. This was my first wakeup call. The second was meeting the eighty-six-year-old pastor there, Lawrence Baldridge, who had a seminary degree and could easily be pastoring a large church somewhere. Instead, he was right there among the poor, the black-lung coal miners. I saw this man and his wife totally giving themselves to these people. I saw what the Christian life was supposed to be. And I saw the selfishness in me, me, me. Deep down I had thought I was a good guy. I always shared my beer and weed with my friends, but I was still missing something.

A week later in Alabama, the Holy Spirit of God showed me what I had become. I had lost all that mattered in life. I saw that I needed help. One night I cried out to God and asked Him to change me or kill me; otherwise I would do it for Him. I grabbed a Bible, but I was high and couldn't focus. After going to the fridge, I got the beer and poured it out. In the freezer was 1/4 lb. of weed, and I threw it in the wood heater. I had been a wasted trucker and my CB handle was "Lost Cause." But that night I repented, owned up to my sin, and asked God to forgive me. Reading the Word of God, I found hope in Jesus Christ. I was born again by the Spirit of God, and my new life in Christ began.

I used to share beer with my friends. Now I started sharing life with everybody. Jesus died on the cross for us all and wants to set us free today and forever. It's a great life that I wish everyone could experience.

Despite wasting many years and hurting my parents with my selfish rebellion, I'm so glad that my dad, L.J. Blanton, could see me as a new person in Christ and a committed witness of His grace. My dad's last words "lost and dying world" remind me to keep sharing the message that Christ died for us and rose again. You, too, can rise above all the pain of life through His love and power.

Jesus Can...

Ronnie Blanton

On that 1997 night of Ronnie's new birth, he prayed, "If You open any door, if someone asks me to do anything in Jesus' name, preach, teach, share a testimony, give, whatever, I'll do it." Now, he and his family are nonstop amazed at what the Almighty has done. Ronnie has served in many locations in a myriad of ways: bus and prison ministry, working as a deacon and elder, singing/playing harmonica on the weekly worship team, now writing for CWC's Book 3, and always reminding us that it's not about him. It's all about Him.

14

◎ ✝ *My Rescue Story*

▼

by Stephen J. Miller

I was much loved by my parents. As many children do, I failed to appreciate this and rebelled. Looking back, I feel that God has highly favored me. My dad, Bob, was a quiet, family man, skilled at carpentry, and faithful as a lay pastor. My mom, Pearl, was a rare gem: loving, but firm when necessary, and committed to the Word of God through ninety-nine years until her homegoing in December of 2022.

At fifteen, I pursued pleasure. I rejected my parents' faith and considered myself an atheist. I lived for the next high. On January 7, 1971, this all changed. While doing drugs at a friend's house, I felt that I was going to die.

I was terrified! My friend tried to calm me, but it didn't help. I noticed a New Testament titled "Living Letters" on a nearby chair and desperately picked it up, hoping it might help. I read from Romans 9:18-21. God is described as the Potter and we as His clay. This spoke to me.

Somehow, I thought that God might help me, though I knew that I was unworthy. I decided to turn to Christ. I called my dad; it was around 12:30 am. He came and prayed with me. I began to gain control of myself, and he took me home. I couldn't sleep because of the drugs, but I could read. So I stayed up for a few hours trying to read the Bible, and finally I fell asleep. In the morning I felt clean and refreshed. I had a wonderful peace. The "old had gone and the new had come" as in 2 Corinthians 5:17.

Dad gave me 1 Corinthians 10:13 to memorize, which I did. Both Dad and Mom encouraged me to make restitution for my wrongs, which became a powerful faith-building experience. I was determined to seek first His kingdom and His righteousness as in Matthew 6:33. I did so because of deep gratitude for my new life. As a result, all of my material needs have been cared for. He is the faithful Jehovah-Jireh. He has also shown Himself to be Jehovah-Rapha, healing me from the damage I had done to my mind and body. I went on to get a college degree in Pharmacy, graduating with honors.

My finest treasures of course are Julie, the best wife in the whole world, our four amazing children, their wonderful partners, a granddaughter, and another grandchild on the way!

During these fifty-two years as His son and ambassador, I have had many opportunities to honor Him. For example, in July 2014, I shared a kidney as an anonymous donor. It was one of the happiest days of my life!

Three months later I received a thank you card from Daniel, the recipient, who had spent the previous two years on dialysis. When he went for his treatments, he prayed to Jesus to get him a kidney. He said that I was the answer to his prayers. I was elated. *(Editor's note: as of March 2023, Daniel is still doing well.)*

The psychological screening for being a kidney donor included ten questions. The tenth question was, "How would you feel if the recipient didn't take care of your kidney?" I responded, "I'm giving it to Jesus, and He will take care of it." I gave it to Jesus, and He gave it to Daniel.

God continues to do exceedingly abundantly above all that I can ask or think as in Ephesians 3:20-21! The medical personnel told me that I could live fine with just one kidney. They also said that my remaining kidney function would increase but never be more than 70% of my previous level. Seven years after donating, my kidney function had returned to normal. The doctors were practicing medicine, while the Savior was sharing life.

Our local church in Corvallis, Oregon, has been experiencing revival for many years, evidenced in part by prayer meetings six days a week and a week of prayer and fasting annually. This year 500 people came to the final night. During a prayer meeting in January 2023, an elderly lady in our church prophesied. She said that she saw the heavens open and incense (our prayers) rising to the throne of God.

I love this picture in Revelation 5:8 where twenty-four elders are "holding golden bowls full of incense, which are the prayers of God's people." These elders fall down in worship as they present our prayers before the "Worthy One," the "Lamb." This reminds us to intercede for all prodigals and unsaved that they will come to Christ while there is still time. Revelation 5 also depicts the twenty-four elders holding harps in worship. This reminds us to worship Him alone, to exalt His name, to sing a new song of praise to Him, and to trust Him who is fully and forever trustworthy.

As that godly prophetess spoke forth the Word in our humble sanctuary, heaven seemed so close. Perhaps I was given this reminder to share with you, and all believers, as stated in Ephesians 2:6, "God…seated us with Him in the heavenly places in Christ Jesus." We've become entrenched in this passing world. As Colossians 3:1 tells us, may God help us to "seek those things which are above, where Christ sits at the right hand of God."

As adoptees into God's family, 2 Peter 1:3 tells us that you and I have been "given all things that pertain to life and godliness through the knowledge of Him (Christ)." I praise Him, for He has lavished on me one blessing after another! By His grace, I walk with Him one day at a time. He healed my spirit, soul, and body. I love Him and all His Word. No rock will "out praise" me; Luke 19:40. I praise the Lord today, and am planning to do so tomorrow, daily, and forever!

Stephen J. Miller

Stephen devoted his life to the community of Portland, the beautiful "City of Roses," by working forty years as a Retail Pharmacist. His wife, Julie, works for the State of Oregon as an Administrative Specialist. She is a proactive team member and a winsome witness for the Lord of Life.

15

✝ *Lost but Found and Free Forevermore*

by Tha Taw Wah

I was born in a refugee camp in Thailand in 1997. My nationality is Karen, an ethnic group from Myanmar. My family and I settled here in the U.S. in 2011. I started using drugs at a young age and made many bad choices. I hated school and got sent to an alternative school. Fights were routine, and I always carried a knife or a gun. I broke into a house and was on the run from the police, so I hid in the house of a guy named Hank. One Sunday morning, I was bored staying home and went to church with him; he got a ride from Ms. Lori. That was my first day at church. I continued to go to church, while either drunk or high. A few weeks later, the police arrested me. In JV (Juvenile Detention), I joined a Crips gang. My dream was to become a gang leader. After a month, I was released and went back to my old habits. Then in April 2016, I got into a fight with some Nepali guys. One of my friends began fighting with a knife. I held a Nepali person down and my friend cut him. I saw the skin tear apart and the bones inside. I told him to stop or we would get charged with murder. My friend dropped the knife. I took it and ran.

Three days later, I turned myself in. I had been thinking about change. It started when I took a selfie with my mom. When I tried to post it on social media, I saw my mom's sad face, and it broke my heart.

When I went to jail, I had seven charges against me. But God used my situation to remind me of my past life. When inmates tried to steal from me, I was reminded of the times I stole. When I got jumped by inmates, I was reminded of the times I jumped other people. It reminded me of Jacob and Esau. Jacob deceived his brother and was also deceived by his Uncle Laban many times.

One day in prison I called Ms. Lori, and she encouraged me to read the Bible. On that very night, I decided to give my life to God. I had learned that the result of our sin is death. I learned that Jesus came to save us if we trust Him. I began to talk to Him, letting Him know that I did not want to serve a ten-year sentence. But I didn't want Him to release me that day because I knew I would become stubborn again if I was released that day. To prepare for my court hearing, I had to meet my lawyer but he was nowhere to be seen. So, I opened the Bible and found Psalm 46: "Be still, and know that I am God...The Lord Almighty is with us; the God of Jacob is our fortress."

Then I called Ms. Lori and told her to forget the lawyer, and that God is my Lawyer and my Judge.

I was sentenced to five years in state prison. Those were very hard years for me. I was unable to leave the Crips, as the consequences were to get beat up or killed. Finally, I could hear the Holy Spirit saying: "You cannot serve two masters. Are you going to choose Crips or God?" I listed the benefits of the two and chose God because He gave me life. My spiritual eyes began to open so I started to attend Bible studies and online Bible classes.

Soon after that, another Crip asked me, "Why are you acting different"?

I replied, "I am different now because of Jesus Christ; I am not a Crip anymore."

He quickly responded, "You are going to have to explain."

I answered, "Because the Bible told me I cannot serve two masters."

He then asked, "Who is your master?"

I said, "God."

He said, "Who is your other master?"

I said, "Satan is working behind Crips, so your master is the devil."

He said, "Watch your back! You know the consequences of leaving Crips is very dangerous."

I replied, "I trust in Jesus; He will protect me from whoever is trying to harm me."

Jesus Can...

I had dreamed of being a gang leader, but now I just want to lead people to Christ.

By God's grace, I was released from prison after doing only five years. Then He sent me back to Clarkston, and I am serving Him here. One thing I do is teach Bible study every Friday night to gang members. If they don't come, I go looking for them to share the gospel. They don't go to church yet, but I go to them. No problem. I am blessed.

Tha Taw Wah

Tha Taw Wah's picture is omitted for obvious safety reasons.

Tha Taw Wah is a man of convictions, forged in the raw experiences of life that all refugees know well. As an ethnic Karen (from Myanmar), he was born in a refugee camp at the Thai border and as a teenager was granted a refugee visa to America. He faced some major crises here, but Christ met him where he was. Now at 27, Tha Taw Wah is a committed evangelist and teaches Bible study to young people wherever and whenever he's able.

16

✝ *From Death to Life*

▼

by Sara Davison

I was blessed to grow up in a loving, godly family. My grandma was my Sunday School teacher, and with her guidance, I gave my life to Christ when I was five years old. From the time I was a week or two old, I was in church every Sunday, and usually once or twice on a weekday evening as well. In my teens I was active in our youth group. Those Christian kids in that group were my closest friends both at church and at the high school we attended together.

Some of my most powerful memories of that time include listening to guest speakers who either came to our church or spoke at the events or retreats we attended. I still remember their incredible stories of radical life-change, from dealing drugs or being an alcoholic or drug addict or ending up in a biker gang or prison to encountering Jesus and being transformed. My mouth would literally hang open as I listened to these testimonies, I was so blown away.

I was also terrified. Terrified that someone would ask me about my testimony because, as far as I was concerned, I didn't have one. Who wanted to hear a story about some goody-goody who never really rebelled, a rule-follower and people-pleaser who rarely strayed from the right path? I carried the belief that I had no radical story of transformation to share into adulthood. When I became an author, I decided that, if I ever wrote my life story, I would call it *I Wish I'd Been a Prostitute* because how cool would it be to have such an amazing story to share with others? Not only that, but the relationship with God that people who have been through something like that had to be truly incredible.

As the years have passed and I have grown in my faith and in awareness of my own brokenness, I have come to realize that my story of redemption and transformation is no less amazing. Even as a five-year-old, I was as fallen and selfish and willful and in need of a Savior as any drug dealer or prostitute. That God sought and found me earlier in life than many, before I'd had a chance to make choices that could destroy my life or that of others, is an act of grace and mercy as unfathomable as the one that saved any other person who has fallen short of the glory of God, as I had even at that young age.

If the sudden, miraculous transformation of a hardened criminal into a grateful follower of Christ may be akin to that lightning strike of "love at first sight," a lifelong journey of growing deeper in that relationship, from one glory to the next as the Bible puts it, may more closely resemble the love story between two people who meet when they are young and become friends. Gradually, over the years, that friendship develops into a love and intimacy that neither death nor life, neither angels nor demons, neither the present nor the future, nor any powers, can ever break. The beginning of the story may be different, but the ending—a deep, life-altering relationship with the God of the universe, one so deep that He calls us His own sons and daughters—is the same.

Every single salvation story is jaw-dropping, but not because of anything we have done or been through in the past. The scandalous idea of a holy God reaching down to a sinful, broken person in grace and mercy, loving that person enough to sacrifice His own Son to redeem her from the pit he or she deserves to spend eternity in, is the testimony of every single person who has given his or her life to Jesus Christ.

That is my testimony. And, all glory to God, it is one of radical life-change—from death to life, from broken to whole, from rule follower to freedom in Christ, from people-pleaser to one who seeks to honor God alone. And it is truly incredible.

Sara Davison

Sara Davison is the author of four romantic suspense series—*The Seven Trilogy, The Night Guardians, The Rose Tattoo Trilogy,* and the *Two Sparrows for a Penny* Series as well as the standalone speculative romantic suspense, *The Watcher.* She has been a finalist for more than a dozen national writing awards, including Best New Canadian Christian author, two Carols, a Holt Medallion, two Selahs, and three Daphne du Maurier Awards for Excellence in Mystery/Suspense. She is a Word, Cascade, and Carol Award winner. Sara has a degree in English Literature from Queen's University. She currently resides in Ontario, Canada, with her husband Michael and their three children, all of whom she (literally) looks up to. Her favorite way to spend the days (and nights) is drinking coffee and making stuff up. Get to know Sara better at www.saradavison.org and @sarajdavison.

17

God's Handiwork in Beautiful Hearing Impaired Friends

by Joshua Asuela

Born and raised in "friendly Philippines," I was truly favored in many ways. And I am so glad to have been raised in a Christian family. Prayer was the rhythm of the day, Sunday church was the rhythm of the week, and good role models were the rhythm of life. No, I didn't live in a bubble. I lived by the absolute grace of God, knowing every breath was a gift. I knew that life wasn't perfect, and neither was I. I was conscious of my sins. Yet, I thought my church attendance plus my Christian parents would guarantee I'd be saved from the penalty of my sins. Thankfully my godly Sunday School teacher said, "No, your parents can't take you to heaven. You need to make the decision. You must personally receive Christ into your life."

As a boy, I was sometimes confused, blinded by people's applause and the devil's deception. I had agonized at the thought of dying and meeting God. Those fears were instantly replaced with peace on Good Friday of 1964, when I was eleven years old. The Lord showed me that the sinless Savior had died for me. Romans 5:8: "While we were yet sinners…" When the pastor extended the invitation, God spoke to me. Many adults responded to that invitation to receive Jesus Christ that day, but I was the only young person to do so; I was ready. I confessed my sin to God and asked Him for forgiveness. Spiritual metamorphosis hit me. Matchless grace.

God adopted me into his family that day. I am wonderfully changed, just as He promises in the New Testament, 2 Corinthians 5.17: "If any man be in Christ, he is a new creature: old things are passed away; behold, all things are new." I no longer run after sin, though sin is running after me. It is trying to enslave me again, but that won't happen. Since that day, I have had peace with God who daily strengthens me to serve people. He enables me to share His hope with everyone who will receive it.

God called me especially to people who are hearing impaired. My family has done that for 40+ years in full-time ministry. We use sign language, the silent word, to share God's Word. We started in 1981 in the mountains where we served until 1992. Then the Lord led us here to Davao, the second largest city in the Philippines. He gave us a large dorm and indoor basketball court. This became a boarding school (grades 1-12) for 100+ deaf teens from many locations in southern Philippines. Most families were too poor to pay anything, but Jehovah-Jireh provided: When it's His will, it's His bill. Can you imagine feeding 100 teens twice a day for twenty-eight years? It took about two tons of rice and vegetables per month. It was a daily challenge, but He was/is faithful.

Hundreds of our graduates returned to their homes and villages throughout southern Philippines. Most went back there as followers of Christ. Decades ago, there were very few churches in most villages, and no fellowships addressing the needs of hearing-impaired people. That has radically changed, as the Almighty loves to use wimps. That's us.

I continue to pastor Davao Immanuel Church for the Deaf. Our purpose is to start a church in each location where our graduates now live. In our Davao City office, I teach classes for deaf pastors three days a week, and Bible lessons online for satellite churches. As director of Deaf Ministries International, my wife, Jocelyn, and I now concentrate on rehab for anyone with hearing impairments. We also volunteer in a nearby K-12 public school where we are free to share Christ with staffers and students, while empowering hearing-impaired students to courageously face academic challenges.

God is building His church and has not forgotten needy folks who are hearing impaired. And He is truly using our graduates to reach this new generation. Our staff and family are honored to share the gospel in words and sign language "in deed and in truth" as written in 1 John 3:18.

I pray that YOU experience this new life, my new friend. God's good news is for all people, including you. He died for us all, that we all may LIVE today, tomorrow, and forever!

Joshua Asuela

Pastor Joshua and his wife, Jocelyn, have four grown children and seven grandchildren, all of whom have had significant roles in reaching out to hearing-impaired youth throughout the Philippines. After more than forty years of teaching and serving literally thousands of young people, Joshua can still beat most teens in full court basketball. (It helps that a covered court is about ten steps from his bedroom.) He also loves reading and discovering new ways of empowering high school graduates to make a living in agriculture and animal husbandry.

18

✝ *From Brokenness to a Vibrant New Life*

▼

by Kelly Erickson

I grew up in the suburbs of Detroit. My mother was from a working-class family there. Sadly, she was an alcoholic, as were her two brothers, our dad, and our grandfather. Alcohol was just the surface problem; it covered up deeper issues. My mom was six years younger than her closest brother. This brother had abused her and held her in his manipulative bondage. My mother never really matured beyond adolescence. She was closer to her middle brother, my uncle who had abused her, than to my father, her husband. She allowed this brother access to me to abuse me sexually.

My father was suicidal and weak. He was unable to stand up to my emotionally and verbally abusive mother. He had been physically and verbally abused growing up and was a broken man. So, I spent more time with my mother and unsafe uncle, who spent the weekends, holidays, and vacations with us.

Thankfully, when I was fourteen, a friend invited me to a Bible study where the truth of God's Word, the reality of Jesus as my Savior, and the presence of the Holy Spirit became the foundation for my life. I read the Scriptures daily and talked with Jesus, my Friend, throughout my days. I grew in knowledge of God's character, which provided the bedrock for my later healing. I walked away from sinful patterns by the power of the Holy Spirit in me.

For even more healing to come, I had to name the anger and sin of emotional, verbal, and sexual abuse in my family. My father had not protected me like he should have. My mother did not care for me, protect me, or nurture me, but allowed me to be sexually abused. She neglected her duties of care and nurture, and instead emotionally manipulated and shamed me. She verbally put me down. For many years, I journaled the sins of my parents and the pain they caused in my soul. I named their sins and my pain and brought all that to Jesus.

Jesus was like an incredible mother to me. He picked me up, held me in His arms, and rocked me back and forth in a rocking chair. He showed me the anger He had that I was not protected from verbal, sexual, and emotional abuse. Jesus sang over my soul with words of love, comfort, and care. He sang lullabies of peace, calm, and acceptance. His love poured over me.

Because my mom was the abusive one in the family, God has deeply ministered to me in passages where God is compared to a mother. Isaiah 66:12-13 NASB says,

> *Behold, I extend peace to her like a river, And the glory of the nations like an overflowing stream; And you will be*

nursed, you will be carried on the hip and rocked back and forth on the knees. As one whom his mother comforts, so I will comfort you; and you will be comforted in Jerusalem.

The genuine compassion of God, loving me as a mother, and delighting in me have impacted my soul deeply. I have been healed in my ability to receive motherly care from God. I can be comforted in God, just as a mother comforts her child. I have seen Psalm 27:10 that even if "my father and my mother have forsaken me . . . the Lord will take me up." God says to me, "Can a nursing mother forget her child? Even these may forget, but I will not forget you, says the Lord. Behold, I have inscribed you on the palms of My hands; Your walls are continually before Me" as promised in Isaiah 49:15-16.

Furthermore, I cried out to the Lord that He would do a new thing in my own family. When I looked at all the abuse in my family on both sides, I saw ruin and devastation in the family tree. Twenty-three years ago, when I was pregnant with my first son, I claimed this verse in Isaiah:

> *Then they will rebuild the ancient ruins, they will raise up the former devastations; And they will repair the ruined cities, the desolations of many generations* (Isaiah 61:4).

I prayed that God would do something completely different and new in my family and kids. If my family was like a dry desert—a weary land with no water, I prayed for water.

A few months later, after the birth of my first son, I prayed:

> *Thus says the Lord who made you and formed you in the womb, who will help you, do not fear . . . For I will pour out water on the thirsty land and streams on the dry*

> *ground; I will pour out my Spirit on your offspring, and my blessing on your descendants, and they will spring up among the grass and like poplars by the streams of water. This one will say, "I am the Lord's." And that one will call on the name of Jacob. And another will write on his hand, "Belonging to the Lord," and will name Israel's name with honor* (Isaiah 44:2-5 NASB).

And the Lord has been faithful. He is more faithful than I could have ever imagined.

Kelly Erickson

Kelly Erickson is married with three grown boys. Kelly has twenty-five years of experience in walking alongside others. She loves coffee, hiking, reading, gardening, cooking, and listening to friends. She is a certified spiritual director. Her philosophy in spiritual direction is to invite Jesus to lead in all sharing together. She listens for the Spirit's direction while listening to each speaker. Her ministry training includes a B.A. from Wheaton College, in Christian Formation and Ministry. She has also earned an M.A. from George Fox University in Spiritual Formation as well as a certificate in Spiritual Direction. She is an active member of the Evangelical Spiritual Directors Association (ESDA) and an Enneagram Certified Instructor at Spectrum Training. Kelly founded a ministry called Hills & Valleys. Her website is HillsValleys.org.

19

✝ *A New Creation*

▼

by Karen R. Naidl

I was raised in a Christian home and regularly went to Sunday School. In those classes, the teachers gave students special pins for perfect attendance, and I had a string of those pins to prove it. Sadly, my faith meant very little to me in those teen years. By the time I was eighteen and in college, I took my religion and put it on the far back shelf of my life. My lifestyle showed it.

Even if I really desired to meet the true and living God, my seven science classes at the university would have totally stopped me. Nearly all professors in public universities followed the religion of evolution. They constantly lectured us that "we all evolved from The Big Bang." As self-centered college students who didn't want to live for God anyway, we gladly followed those self-centered, godless professors. They told us we didn't need morality.

The popular worldview in America in the 1960s and 1970s was "If it feels good, do it." I tried it, but it failed to bring me the peace and joy I was looking for. So I studied harder, hoping that getting the coveted sheepskin in my hands would do the trick. It didn't. After graduation, I still felt empty.

One day I went to the card catalog in the library. (Yes, I am that old.) I looked up the word "happiness" and checked out every happiness book I could find, in hopes of discovering the elusive joy that I thought life owed me. The exercise proved futile. Then a friend and I traveled to Milwaukee. We planned to see the infamous musical "Hair." But God had other plans that were full of grace and truth. We arrived too early at the theater, so we went for a walk. It "just so happened" that some Jesus People were gathering there at the same time. What a paradox! Hippies wearing crosses and loving Jesus! So amusing! They were waiting to hear Linda Meissner, a prodigy of David Wilkerson's Teen Challenge.

Hearing her dynamic message that day was totally revolutionary for me. She spoke clearly and powerfully, as if God was talking directly to us, saying: "There truly is a Jesus! He's coming back to earth! You need to receive Him as your Savior and Lord."

Ms. Meissner challenged us to come forward, pray with her, and make that decision. Everything in me wanted to take that step, but there was a fierce tug of war happening. Finally, I released my fingernails that were digging into my arm. I raised my hand and headed straight to the front of the auditorium. I left my date in the back of the building. Moments later, I was praying with those Jesus People, and by faith I gave my life to Jesus Christ, as my Lord and Savior.

I immediately felt an energized newness in my body and soul, but it wasn't until I woke up the next morning that I realized all my wants had disappeared. The constant gnawing to find happiness through temporal pleasures was gone, and in the days that followed, I was filled beyond belief with joy, peace, and a purpose for living.

I longed for others to experience this same relationship that I had found. I helped start a Christian coffeehouse reaching out to woebegone druggies and those lost in the dregs of society. I prayed, read my Bible, played praise music, and witnessed whenever I could. Soon I met Dave Naidl, who was surely God's man for me. Within a year we were married, and joined the staff of Campus Crusade for Christ. *(Editorial note: this ministry is now named CRU.)*

Since then, fifty-two years have zipped by. I've seen the Lord work through the ups and downs, hills and valleys of life. It hasn't always been pretty or easy. For example, almost three years ago I got hit by a severe virus and became septic in the hospital, not knowing if I'd soon go home or Home! After that hospital week, I was released only to suffer a massive heart attack twenty days later. That year was my slow walk "through the valley of the shadow of death," but I was fearless (Psalm 23:4). He was with me, closer than ever. The darker the night, the brighter the Light of Jesus Christ shines (John 8:12).

I look back at the wonder of it all. He who said "I will never leave you or forsake you" has kept His promise (Hebrews 13:5). He also promised in 2 Corinthians 5:17, "If any man be in Christ, he/she is a new creature. Old things have passed away, behold all things have become new." I am evidence of that changed life.

Karen R. Naidl

Karen had big Friday night plans a few decades ago in Wisconsin, but God had other plans named Wilkerson. David Wilkerson was instrumental in winning many people to Jesus Christ, including Linda Meissner who led Karen to Christ that night. Karen and her husband, David, served as ambassadors for Christ for many years with CRU and continue to serve faithfully in their local church in Manitowoc, Wisconsin.

20

◎ ✝ *Making Music for My Maker*

▼

by Luke Riesterer

I was born in 1976. I am forever grateful for my parents who are faithful ambassadors of the King of Kings. They live to love, making our home a true haven on earth for my three sisters and me. When I was seven years old, I understood the gospel and gladly accepted the Lord Jesus into my life.

I soon found a sweet way to share my faith and have been using it for almost four decades—music. My parents already saw this DNA gift, so I got my first guitar at age nine and was privileged to take classical guitar lessons through age seventeen. I played at a wedding at age eleven; I got $25 for that which was cool. When I was sixteen, I started worshiping with my sax at Bible Temple where the team included clarinet, flute, cello, horns, and strings.

Guitar helped me through adolescence and the many ups and downs of life. I'm really glad for this. Yet there is a downside as I'm not always comfortable in the spotlight. Sometimes playing solo is too much because it demands perfection. If you mess up, everybody can hear it.

My sisters and I had the best grandparents ever. They highly valued us and looked us in the eye; they loved everybody. Three memories stand out: 1) Every Sunday for over four decades, they shared the love of Christ at a local nursing home. I was privileged to serve with them there for twenty-eight years; 2) Grandpa taught me to plaster, paint, and renovate, skills that I'm still using today; 3) Grandma always made sack lunches full of veggies and Vita B bread with meat and cheese. Yummy!

I am secure in the strong, loving hands of my Savior. As His ambassadors, we are commissioned to be "light in a darkening world" as in Matthew 5:14-16. I look for ways to do this using music, gospel tracts, and whatever I can.

A few years ago, anxiety hit me early one morning. I had been praying for friends who had cancer but hadn't seen any answers. I was feeling bad but decided to go out and share hope with people worse off than me. I headed for a very needy part of town and had opportunities to pray with several people, including a man named Cody who was really struggling. I led him in recommitting to the Lord. Then I met a man named Richard at the waterfront who was ready for the gospel, so I led him in a salvation prayer. He was very thankful, and I went on with great joy!

Next came the most powerful encounter ever. I saw a man sitting on a bench, crying "Help me!" He was badly injured. He had several tattoos on his neck and hands, and his eyes showed so much pain. I thought, *This is why I'm here*, so I put my hand on his shoulder and asked, "How can I help?" He introduced himself as Matthew. I just listened. His words were filled with pain, both emotional and physical. He had just been assaulted and was also recovering from pneumonia. He was an addict, admitted that drugs were not the answer, and said, "No one wants to be with me." *Not true,* I thought.

I knew that Immanuel wanted him, so I prayed, asking Jesus to totally heal him. Matthew begged Jesus to meet him there. When we finished praying, he was so different and had peace in his eyes. He took deep breaths and said he felt better already. Then he looked out over the Willamette river, pointed, and screamed, "Look at that!" A bright section of a rainbow was over the river! We were so excited, and I reminded him of Noah and the promise of the rainbow. "That's a sign of God's mercy," I said. He then sat up and said his back pain was totally gone!

I was filled with joy seeing Matthew's healing, and I actually started jumping up and down. I told him to join me jumping. He was afraid to, but I said, "Just try." He started jumping with me, startling himself that he could. "I can't stop smiling," he said. Soon it was time to leave, so I advised him to check out the Rescue Mission nearby, which he seemed happy to do. I continued rejoicing, believing that God had worked mightily in his life. My prior discouragement disappeared, at least for that day.

I've had many MDs (Miracle Days) when I've seen our good, good Father using me for His everlasting kingdom. I'm also reminded that we are God's hands and heart to a hurting world.

Luke Riesterer

Luke is a gracious and really good guitarist. One highlight was making a Christmas CD in 2002. He respects Bethlehem but urges people to seek the Prince of Peace who was crucified just outside Jerusalem and rose on the third day! Luke is a faithful gospel witness throughout Oregon. He loves sharing Scripture verses and sometimes distributes water bottles and snacks, which are always appreciated. He has represented the Lord Jesus Christ so well.

21

◎ ✝ *God as My "Why"*

▼

by Lauren McNeese

It's 5:18 AM and my alarm goes off to Misterwives. Today is the day, I have decided. A freshman at Lipscomb University, I do not have a car on campus. But I asked this guy for a ride to Vanderbilt for a follow-up appointment, and he graciously obliged. This gives me motivation, a reason to get up out of bed. I am convinced that today I am going to fall in love, and that means today I have a purpose.

As fast as possible I get up, hoping my roommate is not terribly upset with me for setting such an early alarm. I go to the gym, shower, and do my hair and makeup. I have a pep in my step and a smile on my face.

Not to spoil the ending, but things don't work out with this guy. Or the next one. Or the next one.

Later I would sit in the university counseling center and explain to my therapist that I am feeling depressed. So and so rejected me, and while he was nice about it, what do I have to look forward to now? Why am I doing my makeup? Why am I going to the gym? Why do I care?

What my therapist explains to me changes my perspective. It changes the way I see the world and the way I live my life; it changes the way I see my purpose.

I kept asking what my "why" was. She said, and I came to see in my own life, "Jesus can give you a purpose. Jesus can be your why. He can be your why when you take care of yourself, going to the gym and showering and doing your hair and makeup. He can be your why when you follow your calling in life. He can be your why when you get out of bed in the morning. You were created with a purpose: to love God, and to enjoy Him forever. You are a beautiful child of the Lord and you do not need anyone or anything to give you purpose outside of Christ Jesus Himself."

Following Jesus means working at whatever you do with all your heart, and this gives you purpose. He can and will motivate you to take care of yourself and work hard, if only you trust that He has a plan for your life and that you will see the fruits of your efforts over time. It was a hard lesson to learn, but I eventually found that giving someone or something the power to give me a purpose is fickle and will not last. But Jesus will give you a purpose, a real and lasting purpose.

Now go be awesome and go to the gym, put on your makeup, and work hard at whatever your calling is. And one day, the Lord will look at you and say, "Well done, my good and faithful servant" (Matthew 25:23).

Lauren McNeese

Lauren McNeese is a sophomore nursing major at the University of Tennessee at Chattanooga. She works at an assisted living facility as a CNA. Lauren is currently working on her memoir, *The Orange Scarf: Notes on Benzos, Testing Reality,* and *How 90 Days in Residential Treatment Saved My Life*. In her free time (which is very little), Lauren enjoys knitting, Cyclebar, reading, and hiking. Lauren is based out of Tullahoma, TN. She prays her testimony inspires and encourages you.

22

✝ *Chosen by the King of Kings*

▼

by Beth Paraiso

When you visit the Philippines, you soon discover that we are a friendly, hard-working, God-fearing people, and my family is no exception. Good-paying jobs are scarce, so over one million Filipinos work abroad as domestic helpers. When I was seven, my mother left us to work in Hong Kong; a year later my father joined her there. They worked there twenty-two years, so we were basically raised by our grandparents. We got to see mom and dad for a short time when they'd come home every two years.

We were able to attend our Catholic Church every Sunday, which was a good discipline for us. When I was a young girl, God was clearly working in my heart. For example, in grade six, I was earnest and eager to get the award of Best in Religion, which came with a Bible as the prize . . . and I did.

Having been born and raised in the province of Cagayan Valley, I moved to Manila after high school to attend college.

Enroute to campus each day (during my second year), I passed by a JIL (Jesus is Lord) church. It is a popular denomination there. One day I decided to attend their church service. Strangely, on the way there, the jeepney (public transportation that holds sixteen to eighteen people) broke down. The driver had a problem getting the jeepney to start again. After around fifteen minutes of trying, he told all the passengers to get out and find another jeepney. When I got out, voila, there was a church just twenty steps away. Instead of getting another jeepney, I went in to New Hope Christian Fellowship. Perfect timing; they had just started the service.

I've never seen or heard of this fellowship, but it was heaven on earth. The people were loving, the music was beautiful, and the Word of God was preached. I was ready and accepted Jesus Christ into my life as Savior that very day. That was August 1994. I was water baptized a month later. Since the day I accepted Christ, I've had a fervent desire in my heart to know Him more and experience His presence.

I finished college and earned a B.S. in Biology, and then I studied for two years to earn a ministerial certificate at Zion Bible School in Antipolo, Rizal. There I met my godsent man, Jommel Paraiso, and we were married two years after our graduation.

God has been so faithful to us all our lives. For example, four years after we married, we were in a motorcycle accident. I was three months pregnant at the time. We were headed to a prayer meeting that night. Jommel didn't see a huge hole (manhole without the cover) until it was too late. I was thrown ten meters away. When I landed an instant later, car lights were coming at me and I thought, *I'm dead. Those cars are going to hit me.* But they didn't. God's protection was so obvious. We only had minimal scratches and some muscle pain that was gone in two days. Oh! Did I mention that our motorcycle had to be brought to the repair shop? We worried that our unborn child might be affected, but based on a checkup the next day we were relieved that he was perfectly fine. Zion Immanuel, born six months later, has been so healthy and is strong as a horse. (At seventeen, he also eats like a horse!) God has been so good to us.

My husband and I love our teaching jobs at New Hope to Asia Center for Education. All our students come from impoverished homes so it is a great joy to give them excellent opportunities to learn and grow. Before the pandemic, over 250 children from the nearby slum areas came to our church each Saturday for Bible study. We call this group the Superkids Bible Club. Since COVID-19, we've been taking this ministry to their communities.

We are also thankful that my parents and younger brother are now saved and serving the Lord faithfully.

My life verse is John 15:16. I am a sinner saved by grace and unworthy to receive anything from the Lord, but thankfully He chose me and appointed me because He loves me unconditionally. Every year I choose a verse to live by; it serves as my goal for the year with regards to my walk with God. My verse this year is "Set your minds on things above, not on earthly things" (Colossians 3:2). Whenever things don't work out the way I planned, I remind myself to look up and try to see life from God's perspective. I'm a pilgrim passing through this world and headed Home.

Beth Paraiso

Beth and her family are faithful servants of the Lord Jesus Christ in the Philippines. They have been serving together at New Hope to Asia Christian Foundation since 2000. Their son, Zion Immanuel, plans to start college, majoring in architecture.

23

🎯 ✝ *A Serendipitous Life of Giving Back*

▼

by Michael Shepherd

I was born and raised in Alabama where Mom still lives in a huge house with her cat. In fact, I called her this morning to wish her a happy ninety-third birthday. I told her I'd be coming home soon to buy her a steak dinner. She's got a couple piers that innocuously draw me from the craziness of Atlanta. I got home, hugged Mama, reminded her that I'm retired, ate some pie, grabbed my rod (pretended to fish or die), picked a pier, sat down, waited ten seconds, said, "Bye y'all, and zzzzz." Because I worked hard and well for more than forty years, these are my golden years.

I'm not getting old, just more thankful. If someone asked, "Who are you?" my response would be: "I'm a Christian." I'm forever grateful to my parents who worked full-time jobs and sacrificed big time to give us the best education possible. Through age fourteen, we were in church at least twice a week and were privileged to attend Christian school. They diligently taught us about Jesus Christ, lived their faith, and encouraged us to earnestly seek the Lord.

Growing up, I learned to work and loved it. My dad was a skilled craftsman who trained us to work well. We'd tear down an old house with a rope, clear the area, fortify the foundation, and start afresh. Building a house on bedrock is quintessential, especially along a coastline. Thank You, Jesus, for teaching us that in Matthew 7:21-29.

Any fool can destroy; it comes naturally. My dad was a Renaissance man: he loved life and lived purposefully. He never allowed us to tear down a structure unless we had specific plans to build something better in its place. This whet my appetite for blue collar jobs, so I took all the industrial arts classes possible in high school. Some people told me to study at a four-year college and major in sociology, but I didn't need Google to know that sociology grads only made $12,000 a year, not enough. I told them that I needed to eat, not wear a shirt and tie. I graduated from high school in 1980.

God was really good to me during my college years. Being African-American, my kinesthetic learning and teaching style connected me to the world of music. I could play any brass or woodwind instrument. Our college music lab had 40+ pianos and we wore them out. I directed the gospel and jazz ensemble there and minored in music education. God used a fellow student named Joseph to bring my musical talents to life. Joseph was a genuine follower of Jesus Christ and seemingly knew every praise chorus and gospel hymn ever written. We'd jam for hours a day without getting tired. Joe took me to do the music at weddings and churches, and I gained a new hunger for Bible study and fellowship. During those college years I gained a renewed conviction of who Jesus Christ is and committed myself to Him.

Thankfully, I earned college degrees in teaching and industrial arts. For many years, I made good money in construction and enjoyed it. For ten years, I was privileged to teach at one of Georgia's finest schools: Maxwell High School of Technology. My students were fantastic, but sometimes their parents were spastic. For example, one of the sharpest guys started dozing off in class. I met with his mother and quickly learned that she didn't like our school. She told me, "He's gonna be a lawyer" to which I said, "He's gonna *need* a lawyer." I wasn't threatening her, and thankfully she realized that her son would excel in academics and life if she'd give him a choice.

It's very fulfilling to work with teens. I remember one student, Greg Carver, named after George Washington Carver, one of America's finest scientists. Greg came to a one-week summer class in 2010. That started a friendship with his dad, Bob, that continues to this day. In fact, God gave us a vision to start a tech school for international refugees. We planned and prayed about this for three years. Finally, God led Luke Keller (of Lauren Engineering of Dallas) back home to Atlanta to start the Lantern Project as a practical outreach to refugees. With my qualifications of a college degree and field experience, I was Lantern's first teacher. It's now Tekton Career Training and has provided accredited life skills for more than 200 refugees from over a dozen countries, including three Muslim women who studied with their husbands in our electrician track. (You don't need to be 6'3" and 300 pounds to do wiring.) Tekton is in the heart of

Clarkston, considered the "most ethnically diverse square mile in America." I didn't need a passport to serve Christ internationally.

Life is not all sugar. After teaching for many years, I had a couple of strokes. My right hand is still weak, so I don't play instruments much anymore. But I have no regrets.

As a young man, God inspired me to give back, which is how I've tried to live, including teaching in public school for twenty-five years. I simply followed my parents' exemplary life and the words of Jesus Christ that "It's better to give than to receive" (Acts 20:35).

Michael Shepherd

Michael and his wife live in Georgia and are deeply thankful for their three daughters and their husbands, three grandchildren, and many priceless friends they've made through decades of public service. As Michael is the warrior archangel in the Bible, so Michael Shepherd is a warrior for good in America's Bible Belt.

24

✝ *The Last Page*

▼

by Jack Urban

One of my earliest memories is looking down on a busy Manhattan street from a New York City high-rise. As a vigorous eighteen-month-old, I'd crawled partly through an open window and dangled my head over the ledge to watch the traffic below.

I got off to a rough start. Family sickness and other troubles caused me to sink my roots deep in a wild garden. It's painful to think about all the dishonorable things I did, especially during my tweens and teens; I did almost everything wrong. On the outside, I learned to look successful, but on the inside, I was an emotional wreck. It'd be safe to say that the stories of all the ways I messed up and the sins I committed could fill volumes. In hindsight, I see how the Lord protected me during my dark years as I rebelled against the system, authority, and Him. But I began to see things differently after an acquaintance lost his mind after a bad LSD trip, another started carrying a 38 Special to protect himself from the gangs, and track marks on his arms showed me he had added heroin to his list of favorites. I didn't realize it then, but God was at work, and the silent but ever present Holy Spirit awakened a fear that made me dread my trajectory.

Following these and other disturbing events, I began to engage with people I called Jesus Freaks, debating but also listening. After months of hounding from a group of Campus Crusade students, I accepted the gift of a pocket-sized Gideon's New Testament. I read the little New Testament in the evening before bed, and in my nightly reading, the stories of Jesus and his friends took on meaning for me. Those stories that once seemed mere myths transformed into an elaborate history that wove its thread of life into mine.

The Lord was softening my heart like an undercover agent secretly administering a holy antidote for the poison of sin in my life. Jesus became more than a character. I fell in love with His person in a way that differed from the way I loved Bilbo, Aslan, Milo, or even my mother. This strange love came from within, beaming outward like a bright lamp under a blanket. The lamp and the blanket battled for control. As the Gospel tales unfolded in my nightly readings, the God-man's purity, wit, and compassion set a fire in my soul that convicted me of my darkness. I wanted to change, not from forced legalistic fear, but because I wanted to please this character that had invaded my heart. Old desires lost their potency and the voices that tempted me to believe their lies began to sound like barking dogs compared to the music of Jesus. The words of the God-man collided with my self-focused personality as the whispers of Jesus out-sounded the world's clamor. Phrases such as "Treat others as more important than yourselves" and "The greatest among you will be your servant" became my guideposts. A war raged as my old ways and new ways fought.

I have always been a loner, but a new kind of loneliness gripped me on the eve of my first international business trip. As a medical equipment repairman, I learned to act like a swashbuckling troubleshooter. But inside, I was riddled with doubts. Finally, the turning point came. One dark and desperately lonely night, after reading the final words of the New Testament, the power of God removed the veil from my mind's eyes. I knew without a doubt that it was all true—the Bible, faith, Jesus—all of it. I sat on the bed of my California apartment weeping uncontrollably, praying over and over, "Forgive me, I didn't know it was real." To make it real, I signed the last page of the Bible in humility and boldness to state my new faith for anyone to see.

Many adventures followed. I wish I could say I lived a model life, but no, I made many mistakes. The Lord was always there to clean up the mess of my life and set me back on the right road. God knows how hard it is to be human. He is kind and available to laugh or cry with me whenever I reach out to Him. Not everything is repairable, but everything is redeemable, and that's why I love Him. Praise and glory be to Christ!

Jack Urban

Jack Urban is a writer, composer, and artist who finds inspiration in God's little things and how they inform the significant issues of life. Jack is the author of the *Substack Everyday Amazed* (jackurban.substack.com), five books, six music albums (https://linktr.ee/wellspringsmusic), and numerous visual art pieces. He lives near Chicago with his wife of thirty-plus years and enjoys taking his grandson on adventures.

25

✝ *God's Story in My Life*

▼

by Desiree Taylor

I was born and raised in Westerly, Rhode Island. My mom took me to church from as young as I can remember. I am truly thankful because that is really where my journey to figure out who God was began.

I grew up in a Baptist Church, and I went to school with many Catholic kids. I was always watching and listening to what I could, since I wore hearing aids and had a moderate hearing loss at that time. I would ask questions and look to see how their lives were different because they said they believed in Jesus. I really wanted to understand and know about God and who this Jesus was.

I was thankful for my Bible School teachers at church. God placed many sweet ladies who taught me, but there was one very special teacher. Her name was Honor Owens. This precious woman loved on me, prayed for me, taught me scripture, and always took time to know me.

Accepting Christ at nine years old, I was baptized soon after. I was very passionate about my walk with the Lord. I talked to Him often and studied the Bible on my own several times a week. Regularly I went to youth group and church.

I struggled socially in many ways, some due to my hearing loss and others just because I was awkward that way. I didn't really fit in anywhere. This caused me to feel very lonely. I continued to talk to God and go to His Word everyday, but I really lacked having someone walking side by side with me as I tried to figure out how to walk out my salvation.

Finally, I came to a place where I just felt this Christian walk was too hard and too lonely. I set out to see if the grass was greener on the other side. Taking one turn and then another, seeking the love and peace I needed so desperately, I fell into one sin after another, landing in a pit so deep, it felt as though there was no way out.

When I hit rock bottom was when I found out I was pregnant. No matter how many people said I should get an abortion, I knew I could never do that. Deep down I knew that I would live with that decision forever. I chose to keep my baby.

One night I cried out to God and confessed my need for Him. I repented of my sins and recommitted my life to Jesus. I heard God speak to me in a very clear and audible voice. He said, "Keep this baby. I will be your husband and your child's father. I will provide for your needs." It was an incredible, pivotal moment in my life. Just like that Father in Luke 15, my heavenly Father received me and began His work of restoration in me.

I began to realize and become aware that the Holy Spirit had been pursuing me, prodding me, and was very active all along the way. God does not force Himself on us, He allows us to go through what we need to in order to come to Him, to realize our need for Him, and yet He waits and does not give up on us. What a patient, loving, and faithful God!

It has been a long road. Layer by layer He has peeled off so much of me and replaced it with Himself. He has answered many prayers by providing me with a husband who loves me like Jesus, one who has become a father to my son and has given me another son as well. He has blessed me with a wonderful church family, those who walk beside me and those I can walk with side by side.

My sweet friend Honor loved me and prayed for me through it all. We stayed friends until she went to be with the Lord. I know her prayers for me were a gift from God and a protection as I walked through my dark days. Praise God for all He has done in me and all He continues to do in and through me.

I truly am a renewed creation because God saw in me what I didn't see. He loved me and never gave up on me. This is my heart for you and for this ministry! May this be an encouragement to you!

> *I waited patiently for the Lord; And He inclined to me and heard my cry. He brought me up out of the pit of destruction, out of the miry clay, And He set my feet upon a rock making my footsteps firm. He put a new song in my mouth, a song of praise to our God; Many will see and fear, And will trust in the Lord"* (Psalm 40:1-3 NASB).

Desiree Taylor

Desiree is a writer, blogger, and speaker and can be contacted at www.arenewedcreation.com

26

◎ † *Journey to My Purpose*

▼

by Cheri Swalwell

I don't consider myself a writer. Not really. Looking back, I see how God started planting the seeds of writing until they began to bloom, giving me purpose. The Fall of 2006 began as very ordinary. The spring before, I had grown restless. I wanted to live a life of purpose for God. I prayed, asking God to use me and our family for His purpose and then waited.

Approximately six months later, I signed up for a women's Bible study that dealt with trusting God. I realized I didn't trust Him which was hard to admit. I asked God to help me learn how to trust Him, gently, because I was scared.

The first whisper of change started with a missed period six weeks later. We had two children, and had chosen careers that allowed for family time, not luxuries. This pregnancy came as a surprise for us but not God.

One day short of my twelve-week mark, I started bleeding. Three hours later, I lost our baby, in my bed, alone. All that kept replaying in my mind was that the plans I had for our child were gone before they had started. Not only was I wrestling with trusting God, but that lack of trust extended to people. The only person allowed into my hurt was my husband.

As the baby's due date arrived, I was still struggling. I love to read and searched for a book that would promise me this pain would one day subside. However, each book I read to offer salve to my wounds fell short. Instead of giving me hope, they left me angry. Finally, in a fit of rage, I yelled at God, "Fine. If I can't find the book that I need for comfort, I will write it myself." I didn't realize what I was saying, not really.

I had always used words as therapy. I had kept a diary since I was a freshman in high school, and since I typed much faster than I wrote, I started writing a fiction book about our miscarriage experience as a way to get out my feelings, without ever planning on showing it to anyone. It was for my eyes only and was very raw.

November 2008, almost two years exactly after we found out we were carrying our angel baby, Tator Tot, we again received the news that we were expecting another blessing, planned solely by God. That pregnancy was nine months of putting into practice the newfound trust I chose to give to God. It was definitely a day-to-day lesson of bringing my fears to God first, then opening myself up not only to my husband but friends and family who wanted to share in our joys and sorrows.

In July 2009, our bonus blessing was born. One fall morning in 2010, God whispered a command, "Finish your book."

I knew immediately what He was referring to. The book I had started as a form of therapy for myself, for my eyes only. Instead of obeying immediately, I chose to talk back, "What do You mean, finish my book?"

In God's holiness He didn't argue with His daughter. He simply replied, "Finish your book."

I chose to obey. In October 2011 I attended my first writer's conference. While there, I was reminded of the promise I had made to God in the summer of 2007 about "writing that book nobody had written." I told God, "If this is the book that You want me to write, I will obey." In November 2014, *Hope During Heartache* was published.

I never set out to be a writer. If you were to ask me if I'm a writer, I would still say no. I am simply a woman who loves God and is choosing to obey Him in this area. I am His secretary and He supplies the content. I love writing the words that He speaks to me. I love encouraging others through words. It is my purpose.

And the best part? While it took more than the miscarriage, it took a life-altering illness of my husband as well as job loss, I've learned to trust God with every aspect of my life. I still wouldn't say that I'm a writer—I'm a secretary for my heavenly Father.

Cheri Swalwell

Cheri Swalwell is a Christ follower, wife, mother, writer, and speaker, in that order. You'll find Cheri encouraging others through her fiction and nonfiction books (www.cheriswalwell.com) or weekly on Cheer UP Podcast with host and friend, Kara Hunt. Whenever possible, she loves spending time outdoors with her husband, three kids, and two dogs.

27

✝ *Waking Up from the Longest Dream*

▼

by Marlayne Giron

I'm Jewish. My entire family is Jewish going back generations, probably all the way to Abraham, nonreligious Jews. God was never spoken of in my home, and I was taught from an early age that it was a sin for a Jew to convert or believe in Jesus. I remember once in fourth grade my mom freaking out over the fact that I crossed myself and dabbed into holy water out of respect while visiting a friend's Catholic church. You would have thought from her violent reaction that I had murdered someone.

When I was in junior high, a curious phenomenon was taking place in Southern California. They were called Jesus Freaks. I found myself being confronted by total strangers (hippies as they were known then) and having the Gospel and Jesus shoved down my throat. I soon figured out that if I said "the sinner's prayer" with them that they'd go away quicker. At thirteen, one of my best friends became one and tricked me into going to one of the very first Calvary Chapel concerts in their new building. I went forward at the "invitation," having no clue what I was doing, but because there had been a promise of a free gift. I came out to the hugs of strangers and a psychedelic Bible that made no sense to me when I tried to read it later. I asked my friend, Dawn, on the way home, if she was trying to convert me, and when she said yes, I told her, "Well, you're never going to do it!" So much for going forward at an altar call and saying the sinner's prayer. Also, at this time the book *The Omen* had come out, and it referenced scriptures from the book of Revelation. I found a Bible at the home where I was babysitting, and it was that book I read in its entirety at age thirteen. It scared the living daylights out of me.

Fast forward four years, and the year is 1977. I'm seventeen years old and lonely/desperate enough to start talking to God. It's Easter which usually means watching *The Ten Commandments* with Charleton Heston, but this year it was different. A new multi-night religious made for TV movie was on, directed by Franco Zefferelli (of Romeo and Juliet fame), called *Jesus of Nazareth*. I wanted to watch *The Ten Commandments*, but my mom wanted to see the new one. She won; it was her house. It was the first time I had ever seen a realistically portrayed biblical movie (using actual scriptures from the Old Testament, which I was ignorant of at the time). I was emotionally sucked in and became enamored of the Jesus portrayed in the film. Then came the crucifixion. I was sobbing, watching the brutality and hypocrisy of the religious Jews, and when the nails were being driven into His hands this thought entered my mind: *If He could do that for me, the least I can do is to give Him my life.* And I did. I prayed right in front of the television set unbeknownst to my mom and dad. The next Sunday I went to a neighbor-friend who regularly attended church and said I wanted to go with her and accept Jesus as my Savior. Her jaw hit the ground.

The next thing I did was to go out and buy a *New Jerusalem Bible* (I figured my parents would object less with a title like that). Unlike the past, now the Bible suddenly made perfect sense! I began reading the Old Testament: Isaiah, Jeremiah, and Psalms, and I was astounded. There in plain sight were scriptures describing Jesus as the Messiah! Intuitively I knew that I either believed all of it or none of it; I couldn't cherry-pick what I liked. I suddenly realized that I hadn't left my Jewish faith, but that I had finally found it! I then got out my phone book, and with my limited knowledge, began calling everyone up and sharing the Gospel with them. I had become the Jesus Freak that I used to ridicule. I became part of the Jesus Revolution. I was on the very tail end of it. Calvary Chapel became my home church, and I still seek to share the gospel with anyone willing to listen. I even wrote a novel called *The Victor* to get the message of the gospel to people who are like I used to be: nonreligious, don't want to be witnessed to, and won't go to church.

Marlayne Giron

Marlayne Giron is a wife and mother living in southern California with her husband, Michael. She is the author of three published works: *The Victor, a Tale of Love, Betrayal and Sacrifice; Make a Wish (Stories Written for Real People Where They are the Star);* and *In Plain Sight,* an Amish/light sci-fi love story. Her author website is: https://thevictorbook.com

mmgiron@yahoo.com
https://thevictorbook.com

Please subscribe to my website and sign up for the newsletter. Breast Cancer | Kvetching with Marlayne (mmgiron.wixsite.com) (Kvetching with Marlayne)
My author page on Amazon: www.amazon.com/Marlayne-Giron/e/B002XZ5UDC%3Fref=dbs_a_mng_rwt_scns_share

28

Why Am I Here? And What's Next?

by RuthAnn Gumm

During the fifty-six years I have lived on this earth, God has given my life purpose over and over again. The cool thing about God is that He often uses me in His plan without my realizing it. My purpose story began when I was conceived and born to young parents who made the difficult decision to place me for adoption. Through my birth, God was fulfilling His promise in Psalm 113:9 to make a childless woman's home full of children. He blessed my mother with three children through adoption and blessed the three of us by placing us in a loving Christian home.

My yearning to be a mother began when I was three years old. For Christmas, I asked for a baby, and upon receiving a doll instead, I was devastated! When I finally became a mom, twenty-four years later, I cherished every moment of my daughters' lives. I coached their sports teams, taught some of their Sunday school classes, and hosted team sleepovers at our home. I was as involved as a mother can be. When my daughters moved off to college, I had no regrets because I had spent every second I could with them, but I thought my purpose had moved to college with them. I was so wrong. God gave me the renewed purpose of being the primary caregiver of that same adoptive mother from the beginning of my life story. For the last eight and one half years of her life on this earth, my mother lived next door to me. During these final years, she beautifully demonstrated to so many women how to age gracefully. God had provided an outlet for my caregiving in the form of my aging mother who was now going blind and whose health was failing. Even her passing was a beautiful expression of God's love to a faithful follower of The Way, but that is a story for another time.

I was eleven years old when God gave me my passion and purpose to become a teacher. That is the only profession I have ever wanted to pursue. After graduating from college, I was blessed with a teaching position. When students entered my classroom for the first time, these students became my children. I laughed with them, cried with them, agonized over their circumstances, and prayed for them. I helped save some, and I lost some. Most importantly, I loved them. After twenty-nine years in the classroom fulfilling that purpose for my life, I retired. My purpose had been redirected. For this time, I was to care for my mother.

I pray often for wisdom and for words. God grants those prayers. Just over a year before my mother passed, God sent the news of another baby who was due to arrive in August.

God knew we would need that little fella to fill the void that would soon be left by the passing of my mother. Also knowing my mother's heart for fertility issues and a love for her granddaughter who was potentially facing similar issues, He granted my mother the knowledge of the upcoming birth of a great-granddaughter before she passed. This child would come to bear my mother's name. Once again, God was preparing the way for us to trust and love Him without us even knowing we needed that. And He was doing that again through a baby.

After my mother's passing, God gave me a passion to read His Word. He didn't give me any further direction other than to spend time reading scripture. I had always obligatorily read the Bible because that's what a Christian is supposed to do. But this was different. As I began to read, I found that the Bible came alive! I couldn't get enough. I might read for four, five, or six or more hours a day, every day. Topical studies became deep dives for Truth. The passion I felt to learn about God's Heart was something supernatural. This lasted for nearly a year and a half with me knowing God had something planned, but He first only revealed the tiny bit of "read and study My Word." When the call from the local FCA (Fellowship of Christian Athletes) area director came, I broke down in ugly tears. I knew the call to be on staff with FCA was the answer to my prayer of "What are You preparing me for, God?" So now, my retirement assignment from God is to share Christ with student-athletes in our local schools and internationally. Again . . . a story for another time.

Why am I here, and what's next? I now understand that my purpose is, and always has been, to spread the Gospel of Jesus

Christ to others. What this looks like has changed over the years. I learned that a Christian never retires, they just receive the next assignment. Once you accept Jesus Christ as your Lord and Savior, the gospel message turns outward to others. Your assignment from God becomes sharing the message with others. It took me many years to get to that realization, but God knew and was using me anyway. It is no accident that you are reading this article when you are. God sends us messages all the time. We just have to open our eyes, ears, and most importantly, our hearts to receive His messages and live His purpose!

RuthAnn Gumm

RuthAnn is mother to two lovely young women and bonus mom to beautiful twin daughters. She is a retired technology teacher, cheerleading coach, and FCA (Fellowship of Christian Athletes) sponsor. Her interests include her precious grandchildren, gardening, serving on missions, and deep-dive Bible study. She is an active member of her church. Along with her husband, Steve, RuthAnn resides in the Commonwealth of Kentucky.

29

◎ ✝ *Who Is My King and What Is He Saying?*

▼

by Mary Emily Mulloy

June 1979. It was hot, steamy . . . and dark! I could hear fruit bats flapping around the banana trees, huge frogs (the size of small cats), and quite a nocturnal insect orchestra outside the screened windows of my cabin. It was my first night in the jungles of Papua New Guinea. I was beginning a two-month jungle camp training program for new missionaries. I couldn't sleep.

My iron conviction about becoming a missionary on this island was wavering for the first time. On this first night as I lay on my bunk bed, I thought to myself, "Are you crazy to think you can do this? What have I gotten myself into? I'm twenty-seven years old, single, and alone." So many intense feelings of inadequacy flooded my mind. I had prepared so long for this. My whole heart was in this move. But now, *How can I possibly do this? Help me, Lord.* And then . . . Jesus spoke very strongly to my heart and reminded me of the Why and the How. "Go . . . teach all nations . . . I am with you always, even to the end of the world" (Matthew 28:18-20).

His words were strong and clear, and I felt His presence like light in the darkness. "Thank you, Jesus. I'm not alone. You are with me and we will do this together." My burden was lifted. Confidence in Him flooded my mind and for the next four years of my term, I never had those doubts again.

With all my heart I wanted to be a part of bringing God's Word to the tribal people of this island who did not have even one word of "God talk" in their language. In fact, they didn't even have a written language. I had somehow made it through the intensive linguistic training of Wycliffe Bible Translators to become a literacy specialist. I prepared to become part of a team that would develop an alphabet in a previously unwritten language and make simple reading primers and cultural stories that would prepare a tribal group to read the Bible that would be translated by other members of the team.

Although I had grown up in a strong Christian family and had made a profession of faith in Jesus as my Savior at an early age, I got on a different track when I hit the university campus. I didn't know who I was or what life was all about, but neither did most people around me it seemed. I didn't want to be different, so I just followed along with the crowd who lived for weekend dates, football games, and parties.

Occasionally I would go to church. This habit had been with me since childhood, but I was tired of pretending. Why was I making the effort? I hated being such a hypocrite. So, one

Sunday morning in my junior year, I decided this was the last time I would go to church. I went to the college class but felt so alone and odd. Afterward, a vivacious girl named Debbie approached me, and we talked for a few minutes. She began calling me regularly. Her persistence bothered me. She invited me again and again to meet for coffee. Finally, I said yes, just to get her off my back.

We drank coffee and she shared a little booklet with me called *The Spirit-filled Life*. On the first page were two circles depicting life. In one circle Jesus was on the throne. In the other circle "self" was on the throne. She asked me which one most clearly illustrated my life. I knew that Jesus was not ruling in my life. I was definitely on the throne. Maybe this is why my life was such a confusing mess? Debbie and I met regularly after this and began studying the Gospel of John. I began to devour God's Word as though I had never read it before. The trajectory of my life changed slowly but dramatically, and I finally came to realize the purpose for my life: To glorify God (not self) with my life.

My amazing husband and I have served in missions for forty plus years. These years have included time in Papua New Guinea, Indonesia (Irian Jaya), and the Philippines, as well as stateside ministry. God has shown me His strength with every challenge of cross-cultural life.

At one time we were serving in an isolated tribal village when our daughter was born. There were no roads into the area, only a grass airstrip. We slept under mosquito nets because our village was centered in the largest swamp in the world. Malaria was a constant threat.

Jesus Can...

One week we were visiting friends near a coastal town when our daughter, who was about eight months old, contracted cerebral malaria. She was quickly burning up with fever and had shaking chills. Our two-way radio enabled us to talk with our mission doctor who told us what medicines to get at a local pharmacy, so Bob hurried to buy them while I continued to bathe our baby in the kitchen sink. The medicine worked quickly along with our panicked prayers, and her temperature dropped that same hour. Walking with the King and serving Him has taught me that He is in my story and that story is really all about His glory.

Mary Emily Mulloy

Mary and her husband have been serving among the diverse refugee community in Atlanta, GA since their return to America in 2008. Wisconsin is home to their gregarious son while their daughter, her husband, and their two adorable children live nearby. Mary loves to try new recipes, read, take prayer walks, and babysit her grandsons. She also likes to share how God healed her of cancer through a radical nutritional approach to healing.

30

✝ *I Just Knew*

▼

by Carolyn Miller

My testimony of salvation is like many of those who are children of Christian parents. I grew up in a Christian home, attending church, and reading the Bible. I never really knew a time when I was not following God.

In my teens, concerned that I didn't have the dramatic conversion that seemed to make the highlights reel of youth group talks, I started to question whether I was even saved. Until one day at a youth camp I was praying and felt that I just knew I was saved, and that the fact I didn't have some dramatic drugs-runaway-prodigal-son experience at the age of fifteen was actually just fine with God. I was His beloved daughter and still am!

I've realized over the years that it's our whole lives that constitute our testimony, and that God is constantly doing things so that we can testify to His faithfulness and goodness in our lives. It's something like this I love to express and explore in my books, and I'm so honored that readers are willing to trust me with some hours of their time to read fiction that demonstrates the truth of God's grace in our lives.

Carolyn Miller

Carolyn Miller is a bestselling Australian author of historical and contemporary romance. A longtime lover of romance, especially that of Jane Austen and Georgette Heyer's Regency era, Carolyn holds a BA in English Literature, and loves drawing readers into fictional worlds that show the truth of God's grace in our lives. Her Regency novels include the nine books of the Regency Brides series and the Regency Wallflowers series. Her contemporary novels include those in the Independence Islands series and the Original Six hockey romance series.

Her stories have been described by *Publishers Weekly* as "a winsome exploration of life, love and faith" and witty "with snappy repartee that rockets off the page" (*Library Journal*). Readers enjoy these books that are humorous yet also deal with real issues, such as forgiveness, the nature of really loving versus true love, and other challenges. Her novels can be considered inspirational, and may appeal to readers of Christian fiction, who want stories of hope and redemption with a twist of Aussie humor.

Find out more and sign up for her newsletters at www.carolynmillerauthor.com

31

◎ ✞ *Father to the Fatherless*

▼

by Harriet Okumu

Born and raised in Uganda, I was a special child to my parents for three main reasons. First, being part of a blended family, I was the first child in their relationship. I was also a twin which is considered a symbol of prestige and blessings in my culture. And the fact that my twin sister didn't survive made me such a treasured jewel. I survived my twenty-eight weeks premature birth, weighing just a pound. Yes, I was their little miracle!

My dad worked for a bakery, so bread was abundant at home, and our needs were well met. I was the true definition of a "daddy's girl." Almost inseparable, we shared many sweet moments—precious memories. Unfortunately, our time together was short-lived as I lost him to suicide in 1992 when I was only six. Dad's death completely turned my life around. With my mom left with eight children to care for, poverty, pain, and suffering hit our world like a raging storm.

Some relatives took some of us to allow Mom time to grieve and get on her feet. I ended up at my auntie's small mud single room in the Mulago slum, a Kampala suburb. While my auntie loved me dearly, life in the slum was not a piece of cake. There were many families sharing a small outside bathroom and yard. I terribly missed my dad and my family and was mostly sorrowful. The children in the neighborhood didn't make it easier either; they often bullied me and made a mockery of my dad's suicidal death. I became a lonely and emotionally fragile child.

Amidst my pain, a ray of hope came when a new children's program was opened in our community supported by Compassion International. I was enrolled in the program and got a sponsor from the US who paid for me to be in school and met some of my personal needs too. Above all, I got the opportunity to hear the gospel every Saturday in our Bible class at the program.

At age twelve, I attended a children's camp where one of the speakers spoke about the reality of heaven and hell. I realized I was a direct candidate for hell. He shared Christ's sacrifice for our sins on the cross and how He paid the price for us to become God's children and live with Him eternally. This was too good to be true, and I was completely sold. I accepted God's forgiveness and invited Jesus into my heart. It's the best decision I have ever made!

Although believing in Jesus did not change my rough home environment, it did change my heart. I knew I had a Father who loves me so dearly, would never leave me, and would hear me when I call. Instead of crying for my dad, I started crying out to my heavenly Father through every challenge that life threw my way.

Integrity, assertiveness, and sexual purity are some of the other values I learned through my Compassion program that have guided my life's journey over the years. With their sponsorship, I completed my teaching degree, becoming the first graduate in my entire family! I'm forever grateful to my dear sponsors Kent and Kimberly Lurvey of Grayslake, Illinois. Over the years, I've had several opportunities to teach children, especially the needy. It's been my joy to love, support, and encourage them in their struggles, pointing them to Christ, our refugee (Psalm 46:1).

In 2010 I got married and I'm blessed with four children. With my youngest delivered prematurely in 2020, I have become an advocate for premature babies and their families. I'm working on publishing my new book, *Hope for Preemie Parents*, to encourage these parents and raise funds for those in poverty. My family moved to the States for my husband to pursue theological training. We founded Restore Africa Network, a ministry through which we serve vulnerable communities in Uganda as well as train ministry leaders.

It has been such a beautiful journey walking with my dear heavenly Father through life's ups and downs. After twenty-five years, I stand to testify that the Father to the fatherless has fathered me well!

Harriet Okumu

Harriet Okumu is a mother of four. She and her husband are originally from Uganda but currently make their home in Germantown, Wisconsin. She is an educator and a passionate advocate for prematurity awareness. She is also the author of *Hope Restored*, and *Hope for Preemie Parents* (both available on Amazon). She enjoys speaking on education challenges and interventions for impoverished communities.

32

✝ *Living to Love*

▼

by Bob Mulloy

I was born into an Irish/German, Catholic, blue-collar family with a sassy, saucy, smorgasbord worldview, once you add brats and beer, which Dad loved, never risking dehydration. Mom was as sweet as the root beer shakes she made on summer nights. She was all heart. For decades she had calluses on her knees, spending long hours in prayer crying out for us.

I respected the sacrament of Communion and often got up early in the summer to bike one mile to church in case one of the Mass servers didn't show up. The route was straight east into the sun which was friendly except once when I crashed into a parked car. That really hurt. I complained, "God, what in the world?"

He answered and let me choose: go home and whine, or get over myself and walk the remaining six blocks. I went on. Sure enough, the two servers were not there, so I could help.

Jesus Can...

Looking back, I'm humbled that the God of the universe saw me. I also credit my folks along with relatives and friends, that veritable village who also saw me.

When I reached the age for the sacrament of Confirmation, I chose the confirmation name "Michael," the warrior angel. I never doubted creation, the Trinity, the virgin birth of Christ, His life, death, and resurrection, and the need for all people to receive Him as the Way, the Truth, and the Life. These were/are undeniable truths. At age fourteen, I entered a Catholic high school monastery twenty miles away to prepare for the priesthood. All the students were guys, and I was reminded that priests can't marry. About the same time, I made a phenomenal discovery: girls! I was sure that I needed a wife someday, which shut the door to being a priest. Then I heard that the Bible says, "It's not good for man to be alone."

I received a full scholarship to the University of Wisconsin, Madison, but it required me to live in a fraternity house with about fifty guys who seemingly drank more than they slept. I tried marijuana a couple of times, but it was strange, so that was the end of that. I recall one party in January 1970 when I was drunk, went outside with no coat, and laid on my back to make a snow angel. I quickly realized I couldn't get up and passed out. I don't know how long I was out, but suddenly felt some guys carrying me back into the house. That episode scared me a little, so I didn't drink for a few days.

When summer came, I got a job putting on metal siding about 100 feet up at a power plant in Two Rivers, Wisconsin. I worked with a native American who was a real professional. One day we decided to race down to lunch. Sadly, he beat me to the stairs, so I decided to hurry down the ½ inch diameter rope. The rope was too thin, and I free-fell the final forty feet and passed out. I won the race but hurt my back. A few months later I got my Vietnam draft number, twenty-four. I would have been sent to 'Nam later that year but was disqualified. A Strong Hand was keeping me alive.

My need for objective truth was chasing me like a runaway Mack truck. I had religion but didn't have a life. Then on June 21, 1971, *TIME* magazine's cover was on the Jesus Revolution. I couldn't believe it: thousands of young people found Jesus and were happy at the same time. Wasn't Jesus somber and didn't He require His followers to be also?

Four months later, I said goodbye to my family and hitchhiked to Oregon. Within three days I met some Jesus People as well as old (about age fifty) Bible believers. They were living the same message. In John 19:30, while on the cross, Jesus said, "It is finished." Done! I learned that we can't do anything to earn eternal life; it's a gift. I had never heard that before. Also, I had never seen guys hugging guys and women hugging women when they met for Bible study, or wherever. I concluded that it was either really weird or really good.

No way I would throw away my Catholic heritage. Yet these people had something that I didn't! I soon realized, through earnest prayer and meditating on God's Word, that I wasn't converted. I hadn't turned from my sin (including self-sufficiency) and received the free gift of eternal life in Christ. The Holy Spirit was warming my heart with the love of God and warning my mind that I was religious but lost.

Finally, on Nov. 13, 1971, at the compassionate urging of a friend named Shar, I confessed my sin to the Lord, and prayed to receive the free gift of eternal life in Christ. I didn't feel any different then. But at midnight I began to read the New Testament until sunrise. Then I slept until noon and spent the day passing out gospel tracts. I repeated this for thirty days and grew like a weed in this new life. Looking back, I am certain that a genuine conversion had taken place. It was metamorphosis, just as 2 Corinthians 5:17 describes.

Fast forward to 2024. I am nothing, I know nothing, I can do nothing of eternal value apart from the risen Christ. As Paul, in Philippians 4:13, wrote from prison: "I can do all things through Christ who strengthens me."

Bob Mulloy

Bob's salvation experience in 1971 is similar to thousands of other Jesus People portrayed in the *Jesus Revolution* film (February 2023). Bob and his wife, Mary Emily, did evangelism and discipleship for twenty-two years in Asia, and since 2008 have been serving refugees in Atlanta. Their beloved daughter and her family live nearby, and their beloved son lives in Wisconsin.

33

✝ *Football, Faith, and the Sovereignty of God*

by David Naidl

Reflecting on over seventy years of life...I have been blessed in so many ways. I've not had to deal with alcoholism or drug abuse, and my family has not been devastated by divorce. God has blessed me with an incredible wife of more than fifty-one years, wonderful children and grandchildren, as well as in-laws who reflect Christ in how they live.

My coming to Christ took place when I was a junior at the University of North Dakota. Miraculously, and I say that with all sincerity, I was fortunate enough to receive an athletic scholarship in football. In high school I was a second team All Conference player on a team that was 3-8 my senior year. God had already chosen my college roommate: Bob, a 6'3" defensive tackle from a small community in Minnesota. He was All Conference on a conference championship team. We became best friends, and both of us started as sophomores: Bob as a defensive tackle and myself as a defensive end.

During the fall semester of our sophomore year, Bob received a knee injury and sat out the remainder of the season. While in the hospital he met a young nurse who he thought would play a significant role in his future. But he soon found out that she was not interested. Having lost his girlfriend and his place on the Fighting Sioux's 1970 team, Bob headed to California during Christmas break with an attitude of "If it feels good, I'll do it." While there, he visited his relatives who had a personal relationship with Jesus Christ. He saw something different in them and wanted that same relationship with Christ that they had. Bob sent me a postcard saying he could not wait to tell me what he had just experienced in California. My thoughts turned to the three Bs that we were most interested in: babes, beaches and beer, especially Coors.

Arriving back at our college dormitory two weeks later, I walked into Bob's room and was shocked. There he sat with a Bible on his desk and something very different in his life. He shared with me that he had committed his life to Jesus Christ while he was in California. I expected his commitment would be short-lived. Thankfully that didn't happen. I saw Bob's life change to the point where I desired to follow the same Jesus Christ that he was following.

I knew I was a sinner, and that I needed Jesus, the same Jesus that had radically changed Bob. I already knew that Jesus is God and Lord of the world, but I hadn't personally invited Him into my life. Finally, one evening on my knees, I asked Jesus Christ to become my Lord and my Savior. God heard my prayer. The missing puzzle piece to my life was found. I had a purpose for living and a reason for getting up each morning that didn't involve just football, academics, or being successful. Having a relationship with Jesus Christ was real.

I experienced a passionate desire to read God's Word, the Bible. Before that time, Bible reading was like reading my neighbors' mail—interesting but irrelevant. Now, God's Word was relevant and alive. One of my favorite verses is John 17:3 where Jesus is praying to His heavenly Father: "Now this is eternal life: that they know You, the only true God, and Jesus Christ, whom You have sent" (NIV). I made the extraordinary discovery that eternal life was not a place or religion but a relationship.

God gave me a desire to share my faith with other people. Remember that missing piece of the puzzle? Well, I had found it, and I wanted to share it with anyone who would listen. When I was a young boy, a local grocery store was giving away free cotton candy to anybody who came to the store. I thought, *Free cotton candy, fantastic.* I got on my bicycle and told all my friends. It was so exciting to tell everybody about this sweet opportunity. In the same way, it is exciting and much more important to tell everybody that "the gift of God is eternal life through Jesus Christ our Lord" as found in Romans 6:23. He found me, saved me, redeemed me, and He can do the same thing for you. All you need to do is talk to Him.

Do you want to experience salvation and new life in Christ? If so, this prayer or anything similar is a good place to start: "Lord Jesus I know that I am a sinner. I believe that You died on the cross for my sins, and on the third day You rose from the dead. Thank you for your death on the cross for my sins. Please make me the person that You want me to be."

David Naidl

David and his wife, Karen, were involved with evangelism ministries for eight years with Athletes in Action, a ministry of Campus Crusade for Christ International (CRU). In 1983 Dave became a vice-president of investments of a large investment banking firm in the U.S. He retired from the organization after serving clients and organizations for thirty-five years. He and Karen continue to invest in ministries around the world as well as lead small ministry groups in their community.

34

Is That All There Is?

by James Koenig

King Solomon wrote the Book of Ecclesiastes on precisely this issue: What is the meaning and purpose of life? Solomon's thesis is that all is vanity, everything is meaningless, because we all die and will lose everything we have worked, lived, and strived for. What is the purpose in amassing a fortune in investments and possessions, if in the end all will be lost? Why strive for a godly life when the common denominator to all is death?

Solomon lists some of the many preoccupations that fill people's lives: partying, pleasure, wealth, education. All these things have a proper time and place in our lives; however, living exclusively for any one of these is pure folly, as these are only temporary pursuits, for when we die, we leave everything behind. A hundred years after our death, who will care about our wealth, social status, or the degrees behind our name? We will be forgotten entirely as dust in the wind.

Solomon closes with this, "Here is the conclusion of the matter: Fear God and keep his commandments, for this is the whole duty of man."

Jesus teaches the same in Matthew 6:19-21:

> *Don't store up treasures here on earth, where moths eat them and rust destroys, and where thieves break in and steal. Store your treasures in heaven .... Wherever your treasure is, there the desires of your heart will also be.*

Jesus taught that only a life dedicated to Him will have any eternal meaning and purpose. Our accomplishments, our riches, our possessions, our works—it all comes to nothing unless we dedicate ourselves to use those things for advancing God's Kingdom and giving glory to God. Jesus proclaims in Matthew 7:24-27:

> *Anyone who listens to my teaching and follows it is wise, like a person who builds a house on solid rock. Though the rain comes and the floodwaters rise and the winds beat against that house, it won't collapse because it is built on bedrock. But anyone who hears my teaching and doesn't obey it is foolish, like a person who builds a house on sand. When the rains and floods come and the winds beat against that house, it will collapse with a mighty crash.*

What foundation are we building our lives upon? Is it the fleeting security of riches, our work, or the accolades of others? While all these things may bring momentary satisfaction, Jesus sees our lives through the lens of an eternal life. He instructs us to build our lives on the foundation that only He can supply, one that will never come to ruin in life's storms, and even in death. Jesus is the solid foundation that will not fail. In serving Jesus, we find our purpose for living.

Atheists claim there is no God. Therefore, there are no moral absolutes, no Heavenly Father peering over our shoulders. We make our own rules, decide our own behavior, and determine right from wrong ourselves. With no God, life is lived in the moment, finding pleasure wherever it can be found, for we have one life to live and then it's over. We've all heard the slogan, 'You only go around once in life. So, grab all the gusto you can.' Seize all the excitement you can, for after we die, nothing is left but endless meaningless, nothingness. Author Kurt Vonnegut echoes this philosophy: "Eat, drink, and be merry, for tomorrow we die." Many people live their entire lives with this mindset. They rush hither and yon and cram as much activity, excitement, and pleasure into their lives as possible, believing that this is the way to have a fulfilled and purposeful life.

The Bible states exactly the opposite – life has profound meaning and purpose, but only if we live our lives for God. In God's view, eternity is more important than the temporal. Jeremiah 1:5 states: "Before I formed you in the womb, I knew you…" Amazingly, before we were born, God had a plan and purpose for each of us. In the Parable of the Talents (Mathew 25), the Master (Jesus) gives each of his servants a number of talents, some less, some more. When the Master returns after a long absence, he gathers his servants and demands an accounting. Those that produced more talents were highly praised and richly rewarded, but those who wasted their talents were condemned: "Cast the worthless servant into the outer darkness." In contrast, the servants who obeyed and furthered the kingdom, the Master congratulates: "Well done good and faithful servant . . . enter into the joy of your Master!" Jesus desires us to use our talents and resources for Him, to further His Kingdom. Abject ruin will come to those who neglect the Master and live only for themselves.

Jesus commands us in Matthew 16: 24-26:

> *If anyone would come after me, let him deny himself and take up his cross and follow me. For whoever would save his life will lose it, but whoever loses his life for my sake will find it. For what will it profit a man if he gains the whole world and forfeits his soul?*

Our purpose in life is to follow Jesus, take up His cross of selflessness and personal sacrifice, and devote our lives to His purposes rather than our own.

Jesus came to earth to lay down his life for each of us. John 12:47 says "For I did not come to judge the world, but to save the world." Friends, think about what this means! Jesus was willing to leave his throne in heaven, live a life of poverty and servitude on earth, and ultimately die an excruciating death for the atonement of our sins so that each of us can be saved from eternal damnation. This is profound. Carefully consider how much Jesus loves us to do this. He laid down His life for us. Jesus regards each of our lives as having immense worth and purpose!

Dear reader, if you have not found purpose in your life, perhaps it's because you have been looking in all the wrong places. Find your purpose in serving Jesus, for then your life rests on the one foundation that cannot fail—the foundation of Jesus and His Kingdom.

While Peggy Lee's song, "Is That All There Is?" dolefully laments no purpose to life, the ultimate goal each one of us should strive for is to hear our Master say, "Well done, good and faithful servant. Enter into the Kingdom prepared for you!" That's my ultimate purpose in life—please consider making it yours too.

James Koenig

Jim is sixty-five years old, has been married for thirty years, and is the father of six children. He is a dentist by profession but has a wide range of interests, including photography, Christian apologetics, reading, writing, fishing, hiking, and traveling. He lives in rural Forest Lake, Minnesota.

35

✝ *A Senior's Journey to Salvation*

▼

by Gregg Bates

Hello readers! I am a sixty-five-year-old African American male who can finally say that I have found happiness, joy and salvation in my life. It took me almost fifty-five years, but I finally did. Praise the Lord!

Born in a single parent home, I was raised by a strong and proud black woman who decided early that she wanted, but did not need, a man to complete her. I was brought up and raised in church, but I decided to stop going as soon as I was old enough to say no.

Fast forward years later, I had two adult children from two different women, one failed marriage, countless relationships, a major bout with drugs, six years in the military, a bout with cancer, a stent in rehab, two retirements, one nervous breakdown, five career changes, and at least thirty years of worship (on and off).

I can say that I have rediscovered the joy of serving God, devoting my life to being as Christlike as possible, and have been taught by one of the most devoted pastors that I have ever met. Also, I have finally found the joy of life and am living without self-medicating or giving my body away to whoever looked the best to me at a particular moment in my life.

The race is truly not always won by the swiftest. Thankfully we serve a forgiving God who never abandons us, even when we forget about Him.

Salvation is truly free, but you must work at it. Thank You, God, for being a God of second, third, fourth . . . five hundred and fiftieth chances.

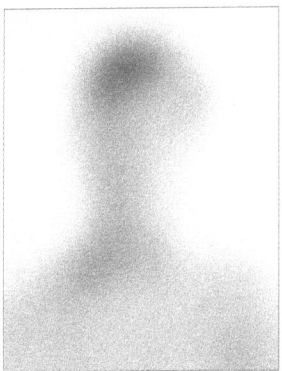

Gregg Bates

Gregg is an aspiring author that lives in metro Milwaukee, Wisconsin. He is a school teacher and also serves the Lord as a bookkeeper and mentor to entrepreneurs.

36

✝ *A Daughter of Promise, A Warrior in Prayer*

▼

by Betzabé

Dios le bendiga! As Hispanic believers, we typically greet each other with these words, translated "God bless you." In the same way, Jews and Christians often greet one another with the beautiful Hebrew blessing "Shalom." I hope my testimony will do both: bless you and bring you peace in Jehovah Shalom.

I was born in 1974 in El Salvador, which means "The Savior." I am fortunate to call "The Savior" my home, even though as a country it has experienced wrenching poverty and countless, needless deaths in this violent 21st century. Sadly, my country was considered the "homicide capital of the world" ten years ago. The situation has improved a little, but there are still over 60,000 gang members and so much heartache and trauma.

I was providentially given the name Betzabé (Bathsheba in

English), which comes from Hebrew "daughter of the oath." I am thankful that God keeps all His promises and perfectly cares for us as His very own daughters and sons. Life has never been easy, but He has always been with me.

As a young person, I was fortunate to have good friends at Bethel Church near our home. I'm thankful for my father, who motivated me to study the Bible, and my Sunday school teachers, who pointed me to Jesus Christ by their lifestyle and teaching. One day when I was thirteen years old, I prayed the sinner's prayer at church and invited Christ to come into my life. That's the best decision I ever made!

I came to the United States in 2003. My parents supported my decision and prayed Psalms 37:4-5 for me. I soon began dating a longtime friend, Saul, and we were married the next year in Georgia. Since then God has given us three beautiful children who fill our home with joy.

In October 2021, I asked the Lord to immerse me in the ocean of His Spirit so I could see the work of His hands. I was praying especially for my husband. Three months later, he went on a spiritual retreat. After that I started to see major changes in his life, and now I can see a fully restored man. We choose to live for God's honor and praise.

A few weeks after that retreat, my family experienced severe testing, which shook us like a sapling hit by a tornado. I began to feel unexplainable sadness in my heart. Was I entering a season of suffering? I called my sister, Ellen, and described how I felt. She told me to cry out in prayer, be vigilant, and trust the Savior with everything.

Shortly after that, I got very sick. It felt like something was shaking my whole body. I couldn't eat. I had nausea and finally went to the ER. I had bleeding from my nose for two hours. But I didn't receive any medical attention. They were busy with other emergencies, I guess. I prayed the whole time in the name of Jesus: "God, come to me; help me, and hold my hand because I am weak and alone." He answered. I had peace and the bleeding stopped. So, I just went home.

A few days later I made an appointment with the gastroenterologist. He quickly scheduled a colonoscopy, which determined that I needed surgery. Medical tests confirmed that I had cancer. Hearing the results, I collapsed and tears flooded down my face. The hardest part was giving the news to my daughters.

I told them, and we cried together. At their young age, their first thought was that they would lose me. I miraculously gained the strength to be their comforter and counselor, reminding them and myself that God was in charge.

I underwent surgery to remove the tumor from my colon. When I woke up I was intubated. It was painful and uncomfortable. I spent the next seven days without food and water; I lived on IV fluids. My husband would come, pray with me and read Scripture, reminding me that I am a daughter of promise as described in Philippians 4:13.

I then received twelve cycles of chemotherapy. My faith was put to the test again. It is not easy to fight against a monster, which cancer is! Many times we have to pass through fire and become living proof for other people that God fights for His children. My victory? I am alive, walking in His promises, and the cancer is gone.

Since February 2022, I often get up at 2 a.m. to pray for two hours. Then at dawn each day, I arise with lifted heart and hands in thanksgiving for a new day.

Betzabé

Betzabé has a powerful intercession ministry throughout Georgia. Many people in her faith community and neighborhood have directly benefited from her heartfelt prayers. She is also a wedding planner and special events coordinator. Her husband is a furniture delivery driver and council member of his church.

37

◎ † *Bringing Light Through Literacy*

▼

by C.C.

I am thankful for my God-fearing parents, sweet siblings, and my Philippines' homeland, which is slightly imperfect but nonetheless breathtakingly beautiful! (I'm a little biased.)

Dad was a rice farmer, and Mom was/is an angelic host. For decades, our three-room house was emptied once a week for Sunday School and then filled with neighborhood kids. We usually filled it up and overflowed outside. The pain and poverty of six days of fieldwork was laughed away on the Lord's day.

At age five, a visiting pastor gave the invitation, and I responded, though I only understood the basics. I just wanted Jesus. Five years later, on May 8, 1988, I recommitted to my Savior. Since then, I've never doubted my core identity as His adopted child; more importantly, His promises have been as rock solid as the boulders in my dad's rice field.

Jesus Can...

In high school, I joined the Light Bringers group in my church. Together we promised to incarnate the blessing of Matthew 5:16 ". . . you are the light of the world." So began my worldview to serve Jesus Christ in missions. Sadly, like many teens, I often found that I was living for self. Thankfully, during my sophomore year of college I got back on track and began to see the Lord use me for His greater glory.

In the process, I quickly learned about spiritual warfare . . . sometimes three steps ahead but two heartaches back. Soon after my college graduation, my dad was seriously injured in a road accident and subsequently lost his vision. He couldn't work the fields anymore, so as the oldest son, I planned to return to the farm. Thankfully, my siblings stepped up to help my mom in caring for my dad, and they encouraged me to continue on my track to serve the Lord.

The next year (2002) I was offered and accepted a job to work with LEI (Literacy and Evangelism International) in producing Bible-based reading primers, an amazing job! Then my best friend, Roldan, died of a head injury. So, I learned to walk by faith and saw the Lord provide all my family's needs and use me in ministry, showing Himself to be Jehovah-Jireh, Jehovah-Shalom, and much more.

An important part of my spiritual formation was living with the Mulloy family for two years in Manila from 2006 to 2008. I was also privileged to earn an M.A. in Applied Linguistics while there, courtesy of par excellence tutelage by world-class personnel of Summer Institute of Linguistics.

I love working with local communities and different people

groups. I make sure that I use my linguistics training in participatory approaches. This engages everyone and allows for heartfelt, meaningful decision-making and a sense of personal ownership in all aspects of community and personal development.

Fast forward to 2023. Looking back, it's been a marvelous life, thanks to Jesus Christ, the Way, Truth, and Life. I've been able to lead teams in research, development, production, and distribution of dozens of reading primers in dozens of languages. The ultimate goal is that people come to know and love Him.

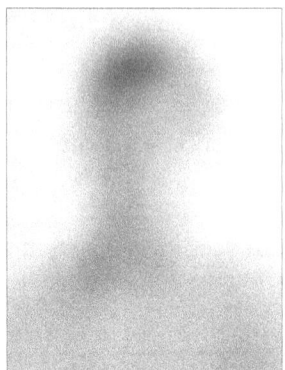

C.C.

For twenty plus years, C.C. has worked as a literacy activist in churches and NGOs throughout the Philippines, as well as serving as a government consultant to implement multilingual education in isolated communities. He is a proactive, proficient, and much appreciated peacemaker.

38

✝ *My Father's Love Changes Everything*

▼

by Danilo Chacon

I was born in Ecuador, but when I was five years old, we moved to New York. We lived in Brooklyn, which was a little crazy.

Our neighborhood had a crime problem. As I got a bit older, we were fighting all the time. Every week I had to throw punches alongside my little brother just to walk down the block. Dad and Mom worked all the time. I walked to school about ten blocks, got beat up many times, and almost was kidnapped multiple times. Thankfully, my dad is a wise man and moved us to Atlanta when I was sixteen. I chose to live my own way, a bad choice. I graduated high school and then moved back to New York.

I was making good money as a commercial contractor in Queens, New York, until the 2008 crash. I lost everything, except my cocaine addiction. I couldn't stop. I tried a few times, but my body would start going through withdrawals that I couldn't take. I didn't eat much. I remember looking in the mirror and saying, "You're an addict; you have no purpose for living." The year 2009 arrived, and my parents realized I had a major problem. One of my uncles overdosed at age twenty-four, and here I was at twenty-three, thinking, *Am I next?* My parents took me back into their Atlanta home and tried many things, but nothing helped.

I was in the U.S. illegally and didn't have a driver's license or work permit. But I drove, had a business, and paid taxes. I lost hope of ever becoming a citizen, so I planned to hang myself that summer. One day in July, I dropped to my knees. With tears of desperation, I cried out, "God, where are You? If You exist, come into my life. I'm sorry for doing wrong to so many people, and I forgive the people that hurt me. I'm sorry, Father." I got up and wiped my tears.

I instantly started searching the house for tools. Maybe God had a job lined up for me. My dad had tools scattered around the house. I went out to the shed, started grabbing tools, and accidently grabbed a Bible that I had never seen before. Then I went to the laundry room, and I noticed a second Bible. Then on to the living room cabinets and saw a third one inside. Then to the kitchen cabinets where I discovered a fourth Bible, all within one hour. I said to myself, "Hmmm, this book wants me to read it," so I hurried to my room. Strange, it was a book with numbers between sentences. And there were all those "thee" and "thou" words in the old Spanish translation that I didn't get at all. Deeply disappointed, I closed it.

A few weeks later, our house suddenly lost electricity, even though no one was using an iron, microwave, dryer, or other electrical appliance at the time. It was weird. I went outside to see if the rest of the block had also lost power. I noticed a U-Haul truck next door, so I walked over and asked the new tenant (Bob), "Do you have any electricity?" They had just arrived that day from Alabama. He went into his house to check. A minute later, he came out saying they had lights, and then gave me a book he wrote on the gospel of John, called *The Light of Life*. I went back to my house, and the power was back on! So, I read it.

A month later, as I was arriving home from work, I saw a lit ambulance at my parents' house. My eight-year-old cousin Jacob had busted his head in a skateboard accident. I did a U-turn and began to follow the ambulance. Neighbor Bob jumped in, and before we left our street, he said, "Let's pray." So, he started praying as if God was really listening. I had been expecting a Hail Mary or something. At the hospital, my nephew received stitches in his head, and the doctors made him stay until morning. I grabbed a soft chair in an empty room, and a chaplain gave me a pocket size New Testament in modern Spanish, the NIV version. I read the gospel of John. It was like the best high that I ever had. I was high on Truth. I couldn't wait to get home and pull out a Bible with both English and Spanish, and a bilingual dictionary.

For the next month I read it a lot and loved every word. About that time, I looked in the mirror and smiled. This Danilo hadn't gotten high the entire month, for the first time in ten years, and I wasn't cursing in every sentence. This Book was doing something to me. I kept it up for four months. I read through the New Testament a few times. Then on January 17, 2010, I was listening to worship music and had an experience that I'll never forget. It was like a new breath of life from my heavenly Father. I felt His overwhelming love for me. In my heart I knew I didn't deserve that, but I would have been crazy to reject it.

After that, I had to tell everyone and their mother about God being real and Jesus touching people today like He did 2000 years ago. I knew that this is what I was missing my whole life. I was twenty-four then and am pushing thirty-seven now. I've not had a perfect life, but my Father in heaven is guiding me.

He's given me a wonderful wife and four beautiful children. I love my local church and try to share the truth of His Word every chance I get. I've also become a U.S. citizen, which is great, but not as great as being a citizen of His kingdom by grace through faith in Jesus Christ (Ephesians 2:1-9).

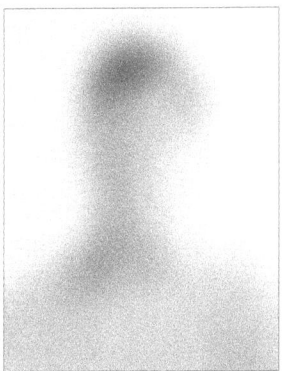

Danilo Chacon

Danilo and Liz have four bright, sweet, and energetic children. They are a great joy and breathe new life into their family and grandparents who live nearby. Danilo enjoys kayaking whenever he can "get on the river." Liz is a busy home-schooling mom and loves serving on the worship team at their local church.

39

🎯 ✝ *Running with the Devil Versus Walking with the Savior*

▼

by Dorsey McDonald

My first birth was in 1961 and happened in L.A. (lower Alabama). I came out a total heathen. As the years went on, I messed up my life in more ways than I can count. I hung out with guys who were about five years older than me, so I picked up all their bad habits from here to kingdom come.

I'm *not* blaming anybody for my bad choices. Alcohol was just too tasty for me to miss, even though we lived in dry-as-a-desert Monroe County. Booze busted my brain and muddled my mind. I couldn't see danger coming.

Education-wise, I got kicked out of schools faster than teachers could line up their ducklings. I never quacked the same as others. At nine years old I knew what juvenile detention looked like from the inside. At fourteen, I was on probation. At fifteen, I should have gone to the federal penitentiary, but I dodged that bullet. At sixteen, I parked in

Selma jail for a while and then went to another school in Clark County where I got a high school diploma.

I never had an I.Q. problem. I had an "I" problem. I didn't want anybody to tell me how to live. When God made the angels, the most beautiful one was Lucifer who used his free will unwisely (Isaiah 14:12; Ezekiel 28:12). Lucifer wasn't the smartest angel; he rebelled against Almighty God and lost. My "I" problem turned me into a loser, following that biggest loser, Satan.

Like most folks in Alabama, we all went to church. I personally tried to make it every Christmas and Easter. I even was married in a church in Coffeeville to a beautiful young lady named Karen Dunagan. I definitely married way up.

I met Karen when I was a senior in high school. We married four years later. Those first twelve years of marriage were up and down, since I was in and out of drugs until 1996 when I was thirty-five. But Karen was faithful to me, somehow keeping me alive. Eventually it got too much for her and our two kids, and she began planning to leave me.

One day I hit bottom and was suicidal. I grabbed my gun and cursed God, as if all my failures were His fault. I cried out, "God, take my life and do something with it." Suddenly He was right there; I couldn't pull the trigger. I instantly realized that He heard me and wanted me alive.

I jumped in my truck and headed to tell Karen as fast as I could. I was filled with the joy of the Lord. Racing down the road, I threw all my liquor and weed out the window. I found her and confessed all my sins and junk to her. I begged for forgiveness. She didn't totally believe me but was willing to try anything, so she let me back in the house. We started praying together, and I finally started doing the right thing.

For the next five months, the Lord and the devil were going round and round, fighting for my soul. Thankfully, two amazing brothers, Shelton Tatum and Chris Boutwell, met with me every Tuesday. They had their hands full. They discipled me as a new believer, and I grew like a weed but without weed. I wanted to share my new life with everybody, so I started doing it where everybody already knew me: the county jail. Since then, I've been sharing God's Word there every week for twenty-eight years. I've helped with several ministries, including three years with We Care.

In my B.C. (before Christ) married years, my wife always wanted to put our tithe in the Sunday collection plate, but I hassled her, saying, "Don't give my money to the man; he only works one day a week." I'm eating those words now as I've pastored in three churches since then and really appreciate Sunday offerings to help pay some bills!

I'm forever thankful for my Christlike parents and sister, Suzanne, who have never stopped loving and praying for me. Many friends also prayed faithfully for me and have allowed me countless opportunities to teach the Word and witness for Jesus Christ. This includes sharing the gospel on seven mission trips to Europe.

More than anything and anyone, I praise God that I lived long enough to see the Light. Among my favorite passages in His Word, Psalm 66:13-20 is glorious. That last verse is true for all people and is a heartfelt reminder to me: "Praise be to God who has not rejected my prayer or withheld His love from me" (NIV).

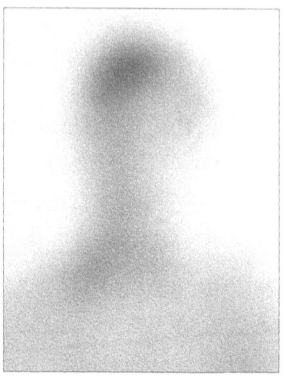

Dorsey McDonald

Dorsey and Karen have been married for over forty years. Their son, Clint, and daughter, Kaley, married sweet spouses who are making marvelous contributions to their communities. Dorsey and Karen are so proud of them and are very thankful for healthy and beautiful grandchildren. Dorsey pastors a local church where Karen is a faithful ministry partner. He continues sharing Christ at the county jail every week and wherever else people have ears to hear and hearts to come home.

40

† *Saved and Kept by Grace*

▼

by Ernesto Rivas

Hola, hermanos. Con mucho gusto! Every breath is a gift, and I'm so thankful to CWC for the chance to tell my bitterSWEET tale of fifty-three+ years. My personal history is His story, except of course when I tried to play God and things went sour. (We southerners don't say, "Things went south.")

I was born into a beautiful and poor family near San Pedro Sula, Honduras, in 1969. Dad hit the road when I was two; that hurt. Mom didn't go to church then, but I did. At age five, I walked barefoot and alone to the nearest one about 200 meters away. Without a dad, I often cried out to God. The other reason I went was that my Sunday School teacher gave us candy if we could answer Bible trivia such as, "Who was Solomon's father?"

As a teen, I was impacted by gang violence that has San Pedro tagged as the "most violent city on earth." At just the right time, thankfully, the Prince of Peace adopted me on

9/11/1988. By faith in Jesus Christ, I gained peace with God (Romans 5).

Because of gang pressures to steal, kill, and destroy, food shortages, and no jobs, I came to the USA in 1991. I soon became very sick, often vomited up blood, and weighed less than 100 pounds. People thought I was dying, but after eight months of rest, I revived! I was already tall and dark but still single, so maybe I needed the extra beauty sleep.

Healthy again, I went looking for a job on my bicycle, was hit by a truck, and needed hospitalization for forty days. I healed up, moved from California to Georgia, and got a painting job. I became active in church and was soon serving as youth pastor, then as a teaching elder/pastor, then as senior pastor. In 2011, I resigned my role as pastor to allow a younger man to reach his generation. I've been doing part time remodeling and part-time biblical counseling since then.

The year 2013 was gut wrenching. My mother had come to Christ and became a powerful prayer warrior, but she died of cancer. A few weeks later, cartel scumbags went to the home of my young sister in Honduras and killed her and her four sons. Two months later, the same men murdered three of my cousins. These demonized killers are still free. Really? No. They're zombie slaves. God reminds us that "We don't wrestle against flesh and blood" (Ephesians 6:12). I pray for those needy men because Christ died for them too. Praying for them spares me from the poison of bitterness.

My son, Ariel, got into drugs for a while and made some bad decisions. But in September 2019, he came back to the Lord and came home to us! He became the son that every dad wants. He went on a short mission trip to Koinonia Farms (Americus, GA) in early November and was reading and loving Bible study. He read the Word many hours a day and then served people in any way they needed. Many people saw clear evidence that his faith in Christ was real and that he was born again. On December 24th, I invited him to church, but he declined. This surprised me, as he loved going to church in those days. As soon as our Christmas Eve service ended, I hurried home, knowing he sometimes experienced depression. Sadly, I found him dead; he had taken his own life. Seeing him, it felt like I was being stabbed in my heart. I had a small glimpse of what our heavenly Father may have felt, seeing Jesus die on the cross for us.

Because of a severe hernia, on October 20, 2020, I had stomach surgery. The docs found more than digested burritos. They took care of my hernia but also found cancer. On the same day, my wife sent me a one sentence WhatsApp message: "I just filed for divorce" and went through with it. I wasn't anywhere near a perfect husband and tried to reconcile but failed. Financially, court fees were painful, but emotionally it hurt much more, especially for our fifteen-year-old daughter.

My daughter was having a really hard time with all that had happened and needed months of residential psychiatric care. She is restored now and blossoming into a beautiful young woman. She had a hard year academically then but graduated from high school in May 2023. Along with the Old Testament patriarch, Job, I can say, "Blessed be the name of the Lord forever."

The apostle Peter walked on water while keeping his eyes on

Jesus, but when he looked away, he started to drown. My secret to keep living is always moving forward with my eyes on Jesus. He died on the cross for us, so I can surely live for Him.

So, if someone asks me, "What's your secret to not faint?" Humbly, I can answer that I don't have a secret, but I recommend the way of a champion.

I've gone through many difficult situations that have marked me. In the process, God has worked to polish my character as a believer, which is His promise according to many Scriptures, including Romans 8:28-29 and Philippians 4.13. I pray that my testimony can be an inspiration to someone.

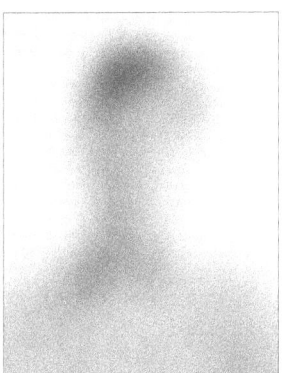

Ernesto Rivas

Pastor Ernesto has been teaching the Word for over twenty years. In 2020 he began a weekly Bible study near Atlanta's international airport. It began through a weekly Bible study that he led for four months where ten people were saved. Despite pandemic challenges, Ernesto has perfect 20-20 vision, keeping the Main Thing the main thing.

41

☦ *My Journey*

▼

by Eymy Chacon

My father is an evangelical preacher, so we were raised in a Hispanic Pentecostal fellowship. My earliest memories were attending church about three times per week for three-hour services. I loved God from a very young age and remember pretend "talking with God." At about five-years-old I recall saying, "Okay, God, take me up there" and then raising my hands for Him to take me up.

As a teenager I struggled with believing God loved me. The church I went to with my parents had strict rules about women wearing dresses or skirts but no jeans. No makeup, jewelry, or cutting your hair was allowed. As a young lady, this seemed impossible. I thought God didn't love me because I didn't follow those rules. I felt judged for wearing pants. It made me distance myself from the only church family I knew.

The enemy used this to make me think there was no point in following God because I would never be good enough.

Jesus Can...

Strangely enough, I always prayed and never stopped believing in God but had no relationship with Him. Prayer was done more out of a religious ritual. Friends and lies from the enemy continued to lead me astray. I would certainly say I had a few rebellious teenage years.

Thank God for parents who prayed and never gave up that I would return to God. It wasn't until I was nineteen years old in college that I started a real relationship with God. It all happened while I was taking a philosophy class. The teacher was an atheist who really pushed his agenda of telling others that God was a myth. He made it sound like you just needed a crutch if you believed in God. Something stirred up inside me that made me want to defend God. I ended up talking with that professor many times about Jesus. It got to the point where he told me to please stop or he would report me to the dean. Looking back, I'm not exactly sure what he would have reported.

This made me start attending church, and I haven't looked back since. I quickly got involved and attended small groups. I learned how to study the Bible and hear from Jesus. This was almost fifteen years ago. God has always been faithful to me, even in those years when it seemed He was far away. He was always waiting for me to come back to him. I know He loves me. I'm His treasure. He bought me from sin's slavery by sending Jesus Christ to die on the cross for me. The price is infinite, something we can never repay.

Life on this broken planet has its ups and downs. As a nurse practitioner, I experience this every day and try to provide the best care for every person. Thankfully, Jesus, the greatest physician, has been my hope and my anchor in all the storms of life . . . ever since I said yes to Him.

One of my greatest joys is our children. When our oldest daughter, Abby, heard that I was working on my testimony, she said, "When I was two years old I pretended to play fun games with God. I told my parents that I had dreams about God. We would be in a gold car, and it was so fun because it went so fast. We also prayed at night. One day in church my teacher asked if I wanted to invite Jesus into my heart. I said yes! The next day, I told God to raise "me up to heaven when I get older." I love God and tell people all about Him, including people in Florida when we go on vacation there.

We are thankful for any time and place to share the gospel of Jesus Christ. Thank you, CWC, for this opportunity as well.

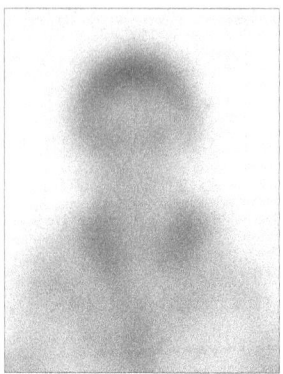

Eymy Chacon

Eymy and her family are at home in Georgia. Eymy's favorite Bible passage is Jeremiah 29:11-12, which appears on plaques, walls, and dressers throughout their house. Being a wife, mom, and fulltime medical professional, Eymy doesn't have lots of free time, but when she does, she loves running and has competed in many 10k events. She says, "Running helps me clear my mind and talk to God or just soak in the beautiful days He makes. It's also a great way to get in good cardio in a short amount of time."

42

✝ *Born as a Refugee, Born Again as a Son*

by Ger

I was born in 1995 in a Thailand jungle. My mother was fleeing the violence in Myanmar. She didn't make it to any clinic in time for my birth, but at least she got out of Myanmar alive. She was fleeing with many others, including a pastor who named me "Gershom" (the name that Moses gave to his son) meaning "I have been a stranger in a strange land." A little later, we arrived at the Mae La refugee camp where I was adopted and given a nickname meaning "the grace of God."

My parents are from the Karen (pronounced careREN) ethnic group of Myanmar. The military dictatorship has been waging war against our tribe and many indigenous groups for over seventy years. Government planes bomb villages of ethnic minorities and plant anti-personnel landmines between villagers' houses and their gardens.

Jesus Can...

Living with more than 100,000 refugees at Mae La camp, I made some friends and became a product of the culture. I wasted my teen years chasing FADS: freedom, alcohol, drugs, and sex. The UN camp provided clothing and shelter but barely enough food and water. Nobody got fat. Unfortunately, we weren't allowed to leave the camp, except in rare cases. So home was like a jail sometimes. I did get an outside job with my dad for a while, doing farm jobs which paid about twenty-two cents an hour. After spending nearly twenty years there, I applied for a U.S. visa and got it. It was hard to say goodbye to all my family and friends at the camp, but I was ready for a change. It meant traveling halfway around the world by myself, which was exciting. I arrived in America on March 31, 2015 at the age of twenty.

I moved into an apartment in Clarkston, Georgia, and started work at a chicken processing plant. I made good money (for a single person) but began to waste it and my life too. I was bored in Georgia and planned to move to a different state. In the midst of those plans, I lost my wallet with my I.D., Social Security number, I-94, green card, and money. All those things are hard to replace, but I eventually got all new documents. I decided not to leave town after all but still didn't have any reason to live.

As a boy at the camp, I often attended church, thanks to my mom. I played guitar on the worship team, but I didn't really worship. I sang for my glory, not for God's glory. I was a Christian in name but not in truth. At age twenty, living in Clarkston, I was the same old person. I went to church, but I was still living for myself. I was looking for love and got married to a wonderful woman, but I wasn't a good husband. Then our son was born. I wasn't a good dad either.

One day I listened to an online preacher who was talking about the many rules and laws in the Old Testament. He said that everyone must perfectly obey all of God's laws. I realized that I couldn't follow all of those laws perfectly. I fail every day, and I'm not perfect. So I couldn't believe that preacher. The Holy Spirit had taught me that we can't save ourselves by trying to follow the law. No religion can take us to heaven, but Jesus Christ can. I remembered the Bible teachings, which I got as a young boy, that Jesus Christ is the way, the truth, and the life (John 14:6). So, I prayed and received Him into my life. That was four years ago in 2020. I've been living for Jesus Christ since then. I am trying to be the best husband and best father.

My family is everything to me now. I love my family so much. I also love my church and our faithful pastor, Daniel. We are very grateful for all God's blessings, including my job. I drive a van forty hours a week, delivering vegetables and fruit, so I meet many interesting people. It's a good job for me because I am home every night with my dear wife and beautiful children. I can also be faithful in Bible studies, youth meetings, and Sunday fellowships. God is taking care of us.

Jesus Can...

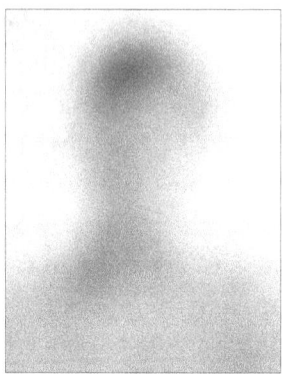

Ger

Ger loves fishing and doing acrylic painting, especially of nature and landscapes. He's never been to his ethnic homeland, so he paints how he imagines it is like. He loves Bible passages about God's creation. His favorite chapter is Psalm 91. He says, "I live my life in every verse of this chapter." Ger and his wife live in Georgia and have three children.

43

✝ *Our Heavenly Father Always Watches Out for Us*

by Norman Chacon

I was born in Ecuador. At three months old, I was very sick and Mom took me to a pediatric clinic. As she anxiously waited for the call to the examining room, two other mothers came out weeping, without their infants that had just died. That was scary. Mom quickly left and took me to other clinics until we finally received an accurate diagnosis: meningitis. Dad sacrificed a lot so I could get excellent treatment. He personally couldn't get proper treatment for his leg injury (twenty-five years prior) as a toddler, so he was determined to provide the best for me. I fully recovered and am forever thankful to my parents for their perseverance. God was loving me through them.

My parents were rich in character but poor in finances. They worked nonstop to pay the bills, but it was hopeless. So, when I was two years old, we came to America in hopes of a good life. God was watching over us the whole time, though I couldn't always see it.

Brooklyn was our first U.S. home. It started well, but when my brother and I hit the teenage years, our folks realized New York was no longer a good place for us. We got into fights with neighborhood teens, and my brother was getting robbed almost every day on his way to school. So, in 2001, we moved to Atlanta, Georgia.

We got into fights in Atlanta too. It was the only way we knew to deal with conflicts. One day, I fought with a guy at school, and he brought an ice pick to school the next day. Thankfully, the administrators got him before he got me. God was watching over me, and I graduated from high school in 2006.

In 2008, I moved back to Connecticut. I had money but no peace. As kids we had gone to church at Christmas, Easter, and a few other times. When I was twenty-two, my brother Danny accepted Jesus Christ and told me all about it. I didn't know what to think. Some people thought he'd lost it.

Soon I started noticing reminders of Jesus everywhere . . . a Jesus billboard . . . a Jesus tract, etc. Then a friend from high school had dreams about me for three consecutive nights, and they all came true. I started to think, *Wow, this Jesus might be real.* I bought a Bible and attended mid-week Bible studies and Sunday services to understand more. After a month of this new routine, I realized that I wasn't going out anymore and had stopped drinking. At the same time, my dream girl, Eymy had been praying a lot for me. God was now watching out for me through a perfect princess!

Then on a Sunday morning in April 2010, an altar call was given, and I heard it loud and clear. I went forward and invited Jesus Christ to come into my life. A few days later, at the Wednesday service, I went forward again. (This was all new to me.) That night I called Eymy and told her. She said, "Oh, you did it again?" She had come to Christ (just once) the year before at a Francis Chan meeting at Victory Church in Atlanta.

A few weeks later I read that Jesus' twelve apostles fasted and prayed so I did too. On my third morning of fasting, I was driving to work and heard Chris Tomlin's song, "Indescribable," on the radio. I pulled off the road and listened to it. God's love flooded my heart though that song. After work I hurried home, quickly turned on my computer, and listened to "Indescribable" again. God's love flooded me again. I wept tears of joy for His unconditional love clearly shown at the Cross. Then I quickly ran down the steps, hugged my brother Danny, and told him that God had shown up in my room. I felt the Holy Spirit's presence and knew He was real. At the time, I had no words to describe it. Weeks later, I read John 7:37-39, which gave me the words. I began sharing my faith with family and friends there in Connecticut.

I was baptized in July 2010. Sadly, I had been having bad headaches for several months. Based on our phone conversations, my girlfriend Eymy, a medical student, diagnosed my condition in October as acromegaly, and she was right. She is the smartest, most beautiful woman I've ever met! She encouraged me to quickly move back to Atlanta, but I was reluctant. Then in November, her Atlanta pastor, Dennis Rouse, gave a powerful message entitled "Move." My heavenly Father had squealed to my girlfriend's pastor. So, Danny and I moved back to Atlanta the next month.

By that time, my headaches had become excruciating for months. For many hours, and sometimes all day, I couldn't function. Finally, after many tests, in August 2011, Atlanta doctors discovered the cause of my acromegaly—a golf ball tumor in my brain. The sweet calm in all these storms was that Eymy and I were engaged in April 2011 and married on September 3, 2011. Then He officially started watching over us as a couple!

Finally, on September 30, 2011, I had brain surgery to remove the tumor. My health has had its ups and downs. I'm still on hard core meds, and docs say that I need to keep taking them. I'm thankful for progress and continue to pray for complete healing.

Accepting Jesus was the best decision I ever made. God never promised it would be easy. In Psalm 23, Isaiah 43, Matthew 28, and many other Bible passages, He promises to always be with me and has kept all His promises. He has been wonderfully watching over me!

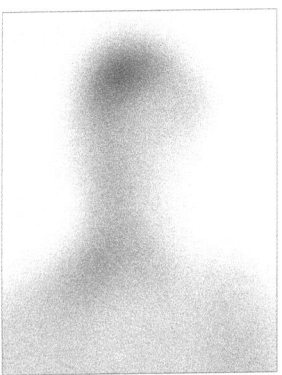

Norman Chacon

Norman and Eymy have three beautiful young girls and are serving their church and communities with compassion, perseverance, and excellence. Norman runs a landscaping business, and Eymy works full-time as a nurse practitioner.

44

⌖ ✝ *The Secret Is His Righteousness*

by Phil Snyder

I was born on April 26, 1958 in Central City, Nebraska. I have three siblings and seven foster siblings, since my dad worked for Child and Family Services. He had a big heart and knew there was always room for one more child in need of TLC. He also knew that Mom was a loving and capable woman.

My folks were God-fearing people, which can be good or bad. We were always in church. I'm not sure why. God was an angry God, or so it seemed now and then.

My family was fortunate to have the Bible as the standard of truth, something that my grandfather spoke and lived. He was a circuit rider, a preacher who had a horse and used it to travel from town to town, spreading the gospel. I personally had a strong foundation of truth as a boy. I came to Christ by simple faith when I was about nine years old, and I'm forever grateful for our Awana program and leaders that were great models for me.

Unfortunately, I have two feet. I always wanted one foot in the world, making dumb choices based on what was most fun regardless of personal consequences to me physically or spiritually. As a teen, I ended up in juvenile detention more than once and did my share of drinking and driving. I married young, but that ended in divorce in 1986. I was an anti-authority dude, so I pretty much drove my dad and mom crazy.

Thankfully, God never gave up on me. In 1987, I came back to Christ and began to live as a committed believer. A major catalyst was the Promise Keepers movement that challenged me and other guys to follow the Lord in all areas of life. In particular, I met and grew to love some amazing African-American brothers in nearby Clausell. The bond we had in Christ was real, unbreakable, and priceless. About that time, He brought a wonderful woman into my life named Becky. I proposed, she accepted, and the rest is glory! I am forever thankful for her.

It was natural to give back, so God allowed me to have a part in several ministries for the past forty years. One is a small group of guys that meet together to pray for each other and other people. Then we hop on our bikes to deliver Bibles and gospel tracts, so we named our group Hog Wild for Jesus. For over thirty years, we've been serving men each week in the county jail as well as the state prison an hour away.

For ten of those years, I served with Celebrate Recovery in

Monroeville, Alabama, thanks to the love and leadership of Pastor Gary and Jane Miller. They got the vision while attending training at the mother lode, Saddleback Church in California. Returning to Alabama, God used them to challenge me to be in CR leadership which I was privileged to do.

Our Celebrate supper was every Tuesday night at the First Baptist Church. Cooking with Becky, we'd welcome whoever the Lord and the county judge would send us. The food was really good, and there was always plenty of it. After the meal, we'd have singing, sharing, and then small group sharing time for whoever wanted to say something. It was casual, but directed by the Lord, so we saw many lives turned around for the good.

I remember a big, angry guy named Cobb whom the judge sent over. He didn't want to be there, but it was either us or jail. Wayne Holley made him feel welcome and spent time with him. One night Cobb confessed, "I'm tired of living crazy, and I want what you got." He opened his heart to the Lord and became a new man. Then he married a sweet Christian lady. Seeing lives changed like Cobb's makes the effort, time, and tears worth it all.

Did I mention that this spiritual warfare for needy souls hasn't been a bed of roses? Sometimes it was five steps ahead, and four back, or five back. Speaking of back, I've lived with back and neck pain for as long as I can remember. I wish I could forget. It's been a constant companion, forcing me to undergo eleven surgeries. At this writing, two weeks after the most recent surgery, I'm brought to tears of joy and thanksgiving for these two glorious weeks of no pain.

Aside from being a workaholic mechanic, another cause for some of my medical problems was unrighteous living. In the pride of my youth, I did some dumb stuff. But our good, good Father in heaven is full of mercy and lovingkindness. When I returned to Him as a prodigal son, He took me in, amazingly, as always. I'm overwhelmed by His goodness in keeping all His promises, including Isaiah 1:18:

> Come now, and let us reason together, saith the Lord: though your sins be as scarlet, they shall be as white as snow; though they are red as crimson, they shall be like wool.

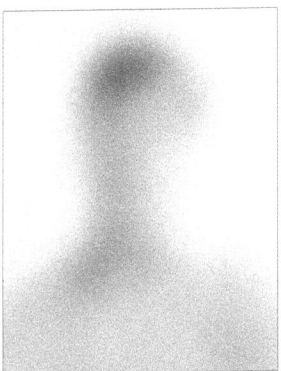

Phil Snyder

Phil and his wife have been serving the Lord for many years in Alabama. They've also done many mission trips in seven states and still make annual runs to serve at an orphanage in French Camp, Mississippi, and at Beautiful Feet ministry in Fort Worth, Texas. Phil's life verse is Philippians 4:13.

45

✝ *Buried for Three Days but Spared and Serving the Savior*

▼

by Myrlande Laurent

What does it take for a proud person to receive the love of God? Some people come to a clear understanding of that love through a powerful message or a personal witness. For me, it was an earthquake.

Most Haitians make less than three dollars a day. I grew up in a middle-class family so I was comfortable, but I didn't know much about God. I attended Catholic church with my family and was baptized, but I just continued doing whatever I wanted. As I got older, I began searching for the meaning of life, but I was looking in all the wrong places. After I got married, my husband joined my search. We moved to a Protestant church, but we still were not happy. There was much arguing, fighting, and selfishness in our home.

Then tragedy struck. On Tuesday, January 12, 2010 at 4:53 p.m., I was standing at my kitchen sink with my two daughters at my feet. My cousin, Maggie, called me on my cell phone and asked, "How is your grandma doing?" At that moment a violent earthquake shook the ground under my house. My daughters and I fell, then the two upstairs' floors crashed down on us. I must have lost consciousness for about ten or fifteen minutes. I knew that my daughters were buried beneath me. I couldn't move and cried out "Oh God, You've kept me alive. Please get me out of here. Now I know that You are the answer to all my searching. If I live through this, following You in life is all that matters. But if You want to take me on to heaven now, I am ready."

That 7.2 earthquake directly impacted over 3 million people, killing over 220,000, and critically injuring over 399,000. It was terrible. I had to quickly decide: Would this make me hate God, to become bitter or to become better and live for Him? In this, my darkest hour, He met me there. Just after praying, I realized that I was still holding my cell phone. Everything was totally dark, except for the dim light on my phone. Even though the building came crashing down on me, I still had the phone. I tried calling my husband but failed.

Aside from losing my daughters and being in great pain myself, I had two communication problems: 1. My phone battery was dead; it was in the ON position, but not charging for two days; 2. I didn't know it at that time, but the earthquake had knocked out all of Haiti's cell phone towers. For that entire week, they didn't work. But God was at work and gave me two miracles. I had been under the rubble for twenty-two hours and decided to try texting my husband. My left hand was buried, so I had to text with my right hand while holding the phone with my right hand. It was 3 p.m.

Give You Purpose

Wednesday, January 13th. My phone lit up, the text went out, and my husband answered, surprised and happy that I was still alive. Later on, he told me that he and some friends ran to borrow a tractor to come dig me out. I felt their digging far above me, and called to them, but they couldn't hear me. Ten hours later, at 1 a.m., they found me. I was saved in more ways than one. I prayed, "Thank You, God! Now I know that You see me and love me. From now on, lead me and show me how to live. Take full control of my life!"

He did, but unfortunately my legs were crushed. Thankfully, a New York medical team was there, contacted the U.S. Army, and arranged my travel to Atlanta as a medical refugee. My shattered legs were amputated, and I eventually received prosthetics. My fifteen-year-old son, Marvens, joined me in a few months and was also helped with his medical needs. A local church leased a house that was our home for fifteen months. Then a new friend, Lana, found a potential apartment to rent. We had no money, so I fasted and prayed for seven days. On the seventh day, the apartment manager said he could give us one month free if we'd pay $170 to clean the carpet! So I signed the lease by faith, not knowing how we would get money for food and rent for the next month. I called on God again, and He touched the hearts of the medical team that we met in Haiti. They graciously paid our rent for the next eighteen months.

Since that 2010 earthquake, Atlanta has been Marvens' and my temporary home. As Haitians with TPS (Temporary Protective Status), we are unable to apply for citizenship or feel settled. But we are thankful for good health so that we can work hard. Marvens gets up at 5 a.m. and drives one hour to cook at Chik-Fil-A. He also serves as volunteer youth director at our local church. I am so proud of my son. I work as a French translator and seamstress. I prayed for and was given a custom-made sewing station, so I've started a sewing business making sackcloth (burlap) tunics and rugs. This itchy, drab clothing is symbolic, dating back to the Old Testament when Israel often needed to repent in sackcloth and ashes. As a pilgrim, this is my tent-making ministry. My website is: MyrlandeSAC.com.

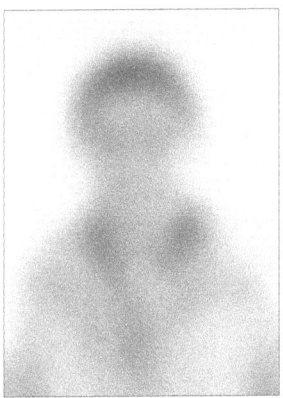

Myrlande Laurent

Myrlande and Marvens love America. They regularly host prayer meetings in their apartment and often fast for three consecutive days. Their prayer is that Christians here, in Haiti, and worldwide will experience personal revival and healing in family relationships. Myrlande's favorite Scripture is from Psalm 116:

> *The cords of death entangled me, the anguish of the grave came over me; I was overcome by distress and sorrow. Then I called on the name of the Lord . . . and He saved me.*

46

⊙ *Destiny Dream*

▼

by Tom Donnan

After inviting Jesus into my heart and life, His purpose for my life began to unfold. Mentally and emotionally, there is a huge divide in comprehending God's spiritual journey for me and the life I was living. This concept is wonderfully said in Isaiah 55:8-9 (NIV), "For my thoughts are not your thoughts, neither are your ways my ways," declares the Lord. "As the heavens are higher than the earth, so are my ways higher than your ways and my thoughts than your thoughts." I was a simple man entering a paradigm I could not see, hear, or understand. I was as innocent as a newly born child. With the Holy Spirit within me, I became spiritually alive and began God's journey.

The spiritual life is conditional, meaning it depends on my willingness to seek God, be willing to learn, and cooperate when being directed to follow the Holy Spirit's leadings. It is a great adventure until the reconstruction begins, then choices are required. Mainly the choice is to yield self to gain

Christlikeness. He is the picture of pure healthiness. I am a dysfunctional mess and often unwilling to delve into learning God's ways and touching life's pains. However, part of the fun for me is following the Holy Spirit and not knowing what comes next. My loving heavenly Father has plans for me, and He releases them upon the pathway to His purpose.

Then came the night I had an extraordinary experience. It was as if I were living this event, this dream. It is nearly thirty-five years later and I can still remember it in detail. Let me tell you about it. The place? I was in the church I was attending at the time. I was watching in the third person from above and behind my position. Watching myself. I was the speaker that day to a gathering of 800 people. I was not on the platform but just in front of the front row. I looked nice in the charcoal gray suit I was wearing.

Then there was a sudden sound. I was not aware if the people could hear it, but I could. From high above the church property, I could hear a roaring wind approaching. It came through the roof right above my head and just before hitting me it made a 90-degree curve and went towards the people. I watched in amazement as the first row fell backward. Then the next, the next, and so on for what looked like twelve rows. It then ended.

I was so stunned by this experience that at first I didn't know what to do. However, I began to pray. I asked God to bring me to the place where He could use me in this way. I didn't know at the time, but that is exactly what He was hoping I would do. My prayers to place my feet upon a path that would bring me to that place began. I wanted to be that man, co-laboring with the Holy Spirit, in a supernatural way as I had seen in the dream. The people, as it is said in Christianese, were slain in the spirit, their lives changed in ways that do not occur in our natural world. This advanced notice of my potential, shown to me in this experience, could bring about a deep spiritual experience to the Body of Christ. Not often do we experience God in a manifest way. It is life changing. Now I want to see it be realized in my life.

To rework a deeply dysfunctional life like mine took time. Yet as I followed, He brought to me needed changes and healing. Then it began as I saw God's responses to prayers in supernatural ways.

Let me tell you about a powerful season in my life in 2004. During the night I felt the presence of the Holy Spirit. It is a calming, loving atmosphere I enjoyed being in. Laying there in my bed half awake and half asleep, I began to see, even though my eyes were closed. Clouds, layers of clouds opened up before my eyes and then there was a face looking at me. *Uh-oh? Do I stay with this?* With God, if you are uncomfortable and resist, He will withdraw from you. It was the expression on the face looking at me that calmed me down, and I stayed in the experience. The smile on this face conveyed to me this: *Oh, I know something good about you!* The face was so beautiful, there are no human words to describe it. As this face faded, another took its place with the same smile. This happened until I saw a total of four faces, then a stream of water. The Holy Spirit came before me. He smiled a wonderful smile. Okay, this is really out there, but I believe I was being called by God, and He had just opened this event for a purpose.

Here is what happened. I had previously joined a Christian

Chat room with a prayer room on the site. I would go in there and wait for a person to come in asking for prayer. From anywhere in the world, they came. Then we would enter a private chat window and pray. What happened next occurred about 25% of the time. No matter where the person was, the Holy Spirit and angels entered their room in a manifest way. The loving atmosphere filled their surroundings. Often, as I prayed, they would seem to disappear, meaning they did not respond. Then would come a message like this: "Listen, I am crying so hard I cannot see the screen." Or they might say, "I have my hands raised in the air to God. I need to go." One of the best responses during this season was from a missionary from Africa. She had been on sabbatical and would soon be going back. She requested prayer. Then she broke into my rolling prayer asking me this: "Who are you?" Now really what do you say to that? I responded, "Just a servant of the Lord." She then said, "I have had people pray for me for over twenty-five years. I have never had this happen to me." The Holy Spirit had entered her room and blessed her in supernatural ways, I believe to empower her for the missionary fields.

For 143 days and hundreds of empowered prayer sessions, I co-labored with the Holy Spirit and four angels. I cannot describe to you how it brought significance to my life. I felt my life mattered. Those touched during this supernatural ministry had their lives changed. I got to be a part of it. I am not done walking my path to see the fulfillment of my destiny's dream. I believe the best is yet to come.

Tom Donnan

Tom Donnan's heart's desire is to share the gospel of Jesus Christ. Life has wonderfully changed for him since Jesus came into his life. Now he works to see others blessed by gaining a relationship with Jesus.

Note from our founder, Stephanie Reynolds:

Tom's ministry is exactly what the CWC needed to connect our readers to a real and caring human being, like Tom, to have an authentic conversation about how a relationship with Jesus changes everything.

If you have questions, I encourage you to reach out to Need Him Global, today. Their website is NeedHim.org or you can chat with a volunteer, right now, at https://needhim.org/chat-now/

Closing Comments

How Jesus Gives You Purpose and God's Plan of Salvation

Congratulations! You've made it to the end of our third book in the *Jesus Can* Book Series. You've now read forty-six stories of how Jesus came into each writer's life and gave them purpose or how He saved them through their salvation testimony.

We want to make sure that we have fulfilled our mission to you before you close this book. The mission of this CWC book is to spread the message of how to have an eternal life saving relationship with Jesus Christ. Our hope is that everyone who reads this book has a personal relationship with Him now. If not, we hope that you start that personal relationship with Jesus by the time you reach the end of these closing comments.

On the next few pages are three simple steps for beginning your new life in Christ just as all forty-six of the CWC members/writers featured in this book have done. Receiving your new life in Christ is as simple as ABC...

A—Accept & Admit

Accept the fact that you've done wrong things and admit that you need forgiveness.

> *For all have sinned and fall short of the glory of God* (Romans 3:23).

> *For the wages of sin is death* (Romans 6:23a).

> *But if we freely admit our sins when His light uncovers them, He will be faithful to forgive us every time. God is just to forgive us our sins because of Christ, and He will continue to cleanse us from all unrighteousness* (1 John 1:9).

B—Believe & Behave

When you believe that Jesus died on the cross and rose bodily from the grave, paying the penalty for your sins, it changes you. That's because when you change what you believe, it changes how you behave.

> *For God so loved the world that He gave his one and only Son, that whoever believes in Him shall not perish but have eternal life. For God did not send His Son into the world to condemn the world, but to save the world through Him* (John 3:16-17).

> *"The time has come," he said. "The kingdom of God has come near. Repent and believe the good news!"* (Mark 1:15)

They replied, "Believe in the Lord Jesus, and you will be saved—you and your household" (Acts 16:31).

For what I received I passed on to you as of first importance: that Christ died for our sins according to the Scriptures, that He was buried, that He was raised on the third day according to the Scriptures (1 Corinthians 15:3-4).

C—Confess & Choose

Confess Jesus as your Lord and Savior and choose to follow His plan for your life.

If you declare with your mouth, "Jesus is Lord," and believe in your heart that God raised Him from the dead, you will be saved. For it is with your heart that you believe and are justified, and it is with your mouth that you profess your faith and are saved (Romans 10:9-10).

Then Jesus said to his disciples, "Whoever wants to be My disciple must deny themselves and take up their cross and follow Me" (Matthew 16:24).

For I am not ashamed of the gospel, because it is the power of God that brings salvation to everyone who believes: first to the Jew, then to the Gentile (Romans 1:16).

Everyone who calls on the name of the Lord will be saved (Romans 10:13).

If you've carefully and prayerfully read through these ABCs, but you still have questions, or you don't feel like anything has changed—no worries. The first test of your faith may be to believe that you've been forever changed because the Bible says so, regardless of your feelings.

Another name for the salvation experience is being "born again" (John 3:7). Some people are spiritually born again with a thirst for God's Word similar to a healthy newborn baby's desire for milk. Other Christian newborns have to cultivate a taste for God's Word. Whether you're spiritually born into that first group, the second, or somewhere in between, it's important to develop the habit of reading God's Word daily. Like that baby needs milk to live, to grow, and to remain healthy, a steady diet of God's Word is essential to the healthy spiritual growth of a newborn Christian too.

There's a long list of other things that a newborn Christian has in common with a newborn baby. While the innocence of newborns makes them so adorable, it makes them incredibly vulnerable too. The same is true of baby Christians. I'm so grateful to the two older women who counseled me on Sunday, April 10, 1983, the day I asked Jesus to come into my heart and change me. While they rejoiced with me and celebrated the fact that if I had died that very moment, I could rest assured that I'd be on my way to heaven, they also warned me that my decision to trust Jesus had made me an enemy of Satan. My new status as a player on God's team was not to be taken lightly, considering how much the devil hates the fact that he will never be equal to God. These wise women warned me that things in my life could get worse before they got better, now that I was saved. It was only a few weeks before I understood exactly about what they had warned me. Thankfully, even a bad day with Jesus is better than my best day as a sinner destined to join Satan in hell.

The summary of the last few paragraphs, the last few pages, and this entire book series is that Jesus can give you a new life; and when He does, it's just the beginning. Get growing as soon as you're born again. It's one of the few decisions in life that you are assured to never regret.

If you still have some questions about this life-changing decision, I'd suggest going back a few pages to the last testimony in this book, "Destiny Dream" by Tom Donnan. Tom introduced me and the CWC to NeedHim.org. We introduce this great organization to you at the end of his testimony. NeedHim.org gives you the opportunity to quickly connect with a volunteer in order to have "an authentic conversation about how a relationship with Jesus changes everything." Volunteers are available 24/7 to help you and "to bring glory to God" —the two best reasons to do anything, if you ask me. —*Stephanie*

P.S. If you have a story to tell, why not share it in an upcoming book of our series? It's easy to apply to become a member of the Christian Writers Collective—the authors of each *Jesus Can* book. Just submit your well-written, 500-750 word testimony using the CONTACT US form on our website, www.christianwriterscollective.com. If selected, your testimony will appear in the next book in the series.

www.ingramcontent.com/pod-product-compliance
Lightning Source LLC
LaVergne TN
LVHW010159070526
838199LV00062B/4423